BREATHE

Katherine Daugherty

ISBN 978-1-64515-576-8 (paperback)
ISBN 978-1-64515-577-5 (digital)

Copyright © 2019 by Katherine Daugherty

All rights reserved. No part of this publication may be reproduced, distributed, or transmitted in any form or by any means, including photocopying, recording, or other electronic or mechanical methods without the prior written permission of the publisher. For permission requests, solicit the publisher via the address below.

Christian Faith Publishing, Inc.
832 Park Avenue
Meadville, PA 16335
www.christianfaithpublishing.com

Printed in the United States of America

To my amazing, wonderful, sweet husband Todd. If we knew then what we know now would you have still taken this journey with me? I would say that with you I would. We have been through many rough nights and days but no matter what we stay strong in faith and in love and get to the other side. I am grateful every day for your love, hard work and perseverance. You are my rock and I am blessed to call you my own…even if putting our story out there is the transparency you so despise.

To each of our children Justine, Grant and Trent. Although you have given your father and I the ride of lifetime you are our children and we would have it no other way. You made us parents, you have taught us patience and grace and given us more joy in the end that you could ever imagine. From those days of play-doh to drivers licenses to diplomas you each make us proud. Never doubt our love for each of you.

To my patient, tolerant, loving, mom Sue Lechien, you have endured my tears, my upsets, my disappointments and been there to support me when Todd worked those long, lonely nights. Forgive me for leaning on you at times more than I should have. I am grateful that you are my mom and that you raised me to love our Savior Jesus Christ.

INTRODUCTION

I am not really sure where to begin, and yet every good book I've read and every author I've studied says, "It starts with one page," "Start a one-page avalanche," or "Just write and see where it goes." So here I am, and this is page one, and we will see where it goes.

A CHANCE MEETING

Todd and I met when we were in high school. I remember the first time I met with him. He was with some friends in a car, and they told me that his name was Adrian. They passed his class ring up through the driver's window with the initials ATD embossed on the inside. This was an attempt, if in some way, to prove their story. Interestingly, I don't really remember caring either way.

Today that guy's name wouldn't seem to surprise anyone, but in the mid-1980s, names weren't quite as rare in form as they are now. Anyway, from that chance meeting, a friendship developed for the next two years until the fall that I was seventeen when we started dating.

As friends, we hung out together mostly in town, cruising the local strip. I was a sophomore in high school, working thirty to thirty-five hours a week at the local Dairy Queen, while Todd was junior at his high school and he worked part-time as well. Occasionally we went to a ball game or to a movie, but we were both busy with school and jobs that we did not have a lot of spare time to hang out.

After we started dating, the trend continued. If Todd was off work, I was on, and vice versa. We were lucky to get one weekend night to hang out. Often Todd would come and pick me up after work. Our most time together was him driving me to get home.

The book *Memoirs of a Geisha* talked about a mother's personality and a father's being that of water and wood. I don't think I had ever been outwardly rude, but I was just completely unsocial. I wasn't comfortable around others or in social situations of any kind.

Todd, in contrast, loved to meet people. He could engage with anyone and talk about anything. He was like everyone's best friend. I think he got his personality from his dad. I, in contrast, was just like my mom—an introvert even in a good day.

They said that "opposites attract," and maybe this was true. Other than our personalities, Todd and I were so much alike. We ended up marrying a month after I turned nineteen and Todd turned twenty the month after. The date to be exact was May 23, 1987.

THE BEGINNING OF A LIFETIME TOGETHER

Our early years of marriage were no cupcake, although relationship-wise we were as normal as any newlyweds. Our struggles were real, although we stayed strong together, determined to persevere. We purchased a 1972 Richardson mobile home with the living room floor that was caving in and was infested with termites. We bought the furnishings for the entire home for under $150. We were met with times of barely having food to having gas to get to work.

For lunches at my home, I grew up eating grilled cheese and a bowl of soup, to continue this tradition, I thought Todd and I would have this kind of tradition for lunches. The only problem was, we couldn't afford to eat them both. Well, at least, not at the same time. But we had a grilled cheese for lunch and soup for dinner or vice versa.

Pete's Pride was our best friend, and if I had to eat another hot dog, I would swear I would turn into one. I can remember many times making Hamburger Helper, the missing ingredient, hamburger. There was also a local grocery store where people often threw change on the parking lot. I used to go there after dark to find it on the ground to buy a twenty-five-cent soda.

Restaurant napkins for toilet paper, laundry detergent doubled for dish soap: nothing got wasted, and everything was used for something. This lifestyle was new to me. Coming from a home where I usually got what I wanted and having never gone without food, the struggle for me was real. Now the consolation? I wasn't going through it alone, but maybe this was what made Todd and me become stronger. Times were tough.

I remember praying often that things would get better, that our lives were not just going to be this way forever, I remember having nightmares. Nightmares of money shortage, would we be okay. But little did I know they would only get worse. I was commuting to Vincennes University to complete my associate degree in social work, while Todd was working on a construction job and gone most of the time over the week.

My days were filled with logged miles and homework, but I continued to attend my childhood church, and Todd as well when he got home. My walk with God was mediocre at best, but I felt that I, at least, went to church twice a week and tried to do my best. I didn't use language. I walked the line. I was a *good* girl, wasn't that enough?

Many of the kids in youth groups I went to had moved on. Some were in college, some were just no longer there. If anything, I had more communication with the adults of the church than anyone my age, I started to get that growing sense I just didn't belong there anymore. I felt alone. Although my parents attended there all the time, sometimes they sat in other pews, I always sat on the back row, I listened, I absorbed the sermon, and I was there.

If I ever grew up thinking any man of God walked on water, it would have been my first pastor. He reminded me then of who today would be Billy Graham. Reverend Adams had a stature that made him tower the world. His preaching would rattle the rafters, and everything he stood for was everything I believed in. I worshipped him. I grew up loving him as a godly father figure, and it was all because of the roots my parents planted. You see, they, too, thought that he walked on water.

Next to my dad, he was another great man, who taught me to love God. After he retired there was some discord among the church and Pastor Adams left. He doesn't know this but it left me with scars.

I had been a cashier at a local grocery store for almost four years when a position in a school was opened, this would allow me to use my associate degree. I jumped on it and began working as an assistant teacher at a preschool for children who had developmental disorders and severe cognitive deficits. After almost a year, the funding failed to go through, and I was told that I would lose my job by the end of the month. By the first week of June, Todd, too, was told that his present construction job would meet a completion at the end of the month. My maternal grandmother fell very ill at the same time, going into the hospital.

For the entire month of June, I was either stressed over the upcoming loss of my job, Todd's job, or the impending mortality of my grandmother—all of which met their end. Todd's job ended on June 26, 1991, my job ended on June 28, 1991 and grandma died on June 30, 1991.

With everything going on, I realized I did not have my monthly visitor, but I assumed it was all the stress. Nonetheless, I scheduled an appointment with a doctor to be sure I was okay.

On July 9, 1991, we found out that I was nine weeks pregnant. Jobless, broke, scared, and having just lost my grandma, and then I was pregnant. I contacted my previous employer to see if I could stay on the health care plan through Cobra. Luckily I was able to have for the sum of $379.00 per month. I didn't know how we were going to pay for it, but I didn't know how not to.

PARENTHOOD

Todd ended up getting a job with his dad through selling insurance while I stayed home. On February 17, 1992, I was set to be induced at five thirty in the morning when my labor started at three thirty. After a stop from the police and nine hours of labor that ended up in a C-section, we had a daughter named Justine at 2:03 p.m.

The first fifteen months were met with over nine ear infections and not having sleep. Justine was a sick baby. During the day, she was as normal as any other baby, but she was often sick. Eventually after taking her to the doctor so many times, she would scream the minute I pulled up at the doctor's office. I was lucky my mom went with me a few times. Most times I left with her screaming, barely hearing what the doctor told me about what I needed to do. "Get the script" was about it. I never had a night off, not once.

By the time Justine was a year and a half old, Todd was still trying to get a better job, one with more permanent guaranteed pay. Through a family friend, he got in at Prairie Farms Dairy. For about a year, Todd made a more than one and a half hour commute one way to work while working more than thirteen to fourteen hours a day.

Justine and I spent most of our time trying to pass the time while he was gone. Finally, we decided to move so he could be closer to us. We signed a twelve-month lease to an apartment and moved to Greenwood, Indiana. We moved in on September 25, 1993. The first year here was the roughest. I had no friends, and I had no one I was close to. I think our friends from back home were in shock, too; we saw hardly anyone this entire year.

I read my Bible and prayed. I prayed often. I prayed for opportunities, I prayed that Justine would sleep through the night, I prayed for a church, and I prayed for a friend. But among these, nothing came. That year was met with sleepless nights, isolation, and loneliness.

> Come to me; all you who are weary burdened, and I will give you rest. (Matthew 11:28)

Today after working with mental health for more than ten years, I can still smell depression as it wafts through the hall, penetrating even the farthest office from the corridor: mine. If I had known then what I know now, I would have sensed the seed of depression aligning itself on the ground ready to protrude like a bean sprout, wafting through that corridor. Only this corridor was not an office; it was my own home.

After living there for a year, we decided to buy our first home and move to Bargersville, which was about thirty minutes south of where we had lived in the apartment. By this time, I was five months pregnant with Grant. Grant was born on February 24, 1995, at 5:53 p.m.

The next three years flew by. I don't remember much because I was so busy with the kids. Todd continued to work long hours. I just threw myself into the home with my responsibilities. The struggle continued.

We now had a mortgage and two kids. Times were tougher. I continued to pray for the kids, for our family, for our lives. We didn't attend church, although I prayed to find one. I still prayed for a friend. My prayers were short, my time for God was on a limited timetable. If I was lucky to have some quiet time, I might be grateful for the silence. I knew God wanted me to pray more. I knew it. I felt him begging me to trust him. I knew the only person who was capable of putting the pieces in place for me was him.

In the book of Psalm, David prayed, "Give me an undivided heart" (86:11).

My heart was divided—one side wanted God, and the other was too busy to make the time necessary to fill that want. On one side, I wanted to trust God with all; on the other, I didn't have time to give him any of it. What did I expect from him when I wasn't making myself willing to allow him to help me?

Justine suffered from pneumonia, as did Grant. Her asthma was a daily problem. Most nights, I slept on the floor beside her as she lay on the couch. I hated to hear her cough. It made me hurt to listen to her, and it went on for hours and hours. The only thing was, the cough meant she was breathing, so I endured it.

Breathing treatments every three hours for years, sleepless nights, setting the alarm clock to get up. If I had a job, I could not have worked. I had no sleep, just a semi-state of dozing. Countless hours I lay on the floor, countless hours my prayer was make the coughing stop but not if it means she stops breathing. Silently as I lay cold on the floor, very uncomfortable, emotionally and physically drained, the tears fell.

One-night sleep was all I wished for so I could do it another, but that night never came. Over and over and over, I just did it. There was no one else to get up, to take over, so I did it. Justine's breaths depended on me; I would not let her down.

A bit fast forward but when Justine was seventeen, she developed a mass in her right jaw, just along the jaw line. It was March of her junior year in high school. I took her immediately to her pediatrician who quietly calmed our nerves telling us it was likely a swollen lymph node and sent her home with some antibiotics. Over the next few months we went from her PCP to an ENT, she had numerous painful aspirations done as well as antibiotic changes. Justine was dizzy, nauseous, confused, tearful and blacking out. Every time she would drive somewhere we would get a call that she could not drive home. Her dad and I would load up and one of us would drive her home crying, shaking and confused while the other followed behind in her car. This went on for weeks. Finally, one day mid-June the ENT told us that she would need to come in for another aspiration. I said no. I was told that I would be reported to CPS for medical neglect to which I told the nurse go for it. I called her PCP and by the end of the month we were in Riley with a surgeon. By now the symptoms were worse and the pea size lump was the size of a golf ball (you could not see it protruding that much through the skin). On August eleven she had the tumor removed. Yes, a tumor (benign). A two hour scheduled to end surgery at seven p.m. ended at around one a.m. and lasted almost seven. Due to the intricacy of the facial nerves, the location and growth of tumor it took this many hours. Justine was given a facelift scar. At the age of twenty-six today she still battles the emotional side this left. The pain, the months of the inability to control the blackouts and panic left her suffering the residual effects.

> How long, Lord? Will you forget me forever? How long will you hide your face from me? How long must I wrestle with my thoughts that day after day have grown in my heart? How long will my enemy triumph over me? (Psalm 13:12)

Remember those nightmares? Well, they continued. I dreamed that we were still living in the trailer and that since it was on rollers, we were sinking into the water. I had nightmares of termites, the floor caving in. My nightmares with this house were even bigger. I dreamed of a pink slip, of losing our home, of being homeless, of Justine's health. Groceries seemed trivial at this time. I was more concerned with a roof over our heads with heat, with life. The struggle was real.

At the end of the day, when all the toys were neatly packed and the dishes all washed, I'd sit on my favorite rocker. A small night light illuminated the open living area. I would rock silently as the tears fell from my eyes. My heart, although so full of love for the kids, was empty. In those moments, I felt so alone. I can remember it like it was yesterday. I remember feeling hollow. I remember literally feeling the skin dripping on my skeleton like I was just a piece of flesh hanging on a bone. I wrote this that very night:

Who am I but a shadow?

Cast upon the wall of someone who existed, once upon a time.

Nothing but a mere silhouette, cut, carved… casting…

Who am I but a stranger?

Simply passing through…fitting in nowhere, no place.

A drifter passing in the night.

Who am I but a skeleton?

The flesh upon bone that once held promise is now all but gone.

A hollow shell unable to feel, to enjoy, to pursue.

Who am I that I fear so much? That I am afraid of everything?

Why did my strength, my vitality, my desires go?

Remind me that I am still here, that I need not be afraid.

What is this shadow that I once upon a time was?

I see it now, once a shadow of confidence.

Who was this stranger that I was, once upon a time?

I found a place to exist, to be, to belong.

Where is the skeleton that once upon a time was all that I could feel?

I feel, flesh, muscle, strength, control.

I was now pregnant with baby number three and diagnosed with placenta previa. This was going to be the *problem*: pregnancy. It was October 1997, and Todd's parents had moved to Las Vegas that summer. We hadn't seen them much since our initial move up to north in 1993, but now we were lucky to see them once a year.

Near the end of October, Todd's dad suffered a massive heart attack. There was nothing to do but to figure out how to get him on a plane. So we took out a credit card, and he was on the first flight out within the next twenty-four hours. By then, I was in a high-risk pregnancy. I was six months along and had two kids. I was alone. Todd was gone about a week and then flew home, and then within twenty-four hours, the call came in—his dad was having a triple bypass that morning.

Back on the plane, Todd's clothes weren't even unpacked. I was alone and helpless again. On December 7, 1997, I ended up in preterm labor. I lay in a hospital bed more than seventy miles from Justine and Grant. I lay on the bed, getting painful injections in my hips every six hours. After three days, labor had stopped, and I was sent home.

We continued to live in Bargersville, and on January 16, 1998, Trenton was born at 9:07 in the morning. To save money, I breastfed Grant, and now I was doing the same thing for Trent. Money was so tight that we couldn't afford anything. I stayed home all the time; if I went anywhere, that meant spending money—money that wasn't there.

Justine had started kindergarten and was turning six in February. Within one week of her birthday, Grant would be turning three. We ended up finding a church near us that a woman from our hometown attended. She asked us to come, and so we did. We ended up attending this church for about four years.

I signed up to teach Sunday school and volunteered for Bible school; I threw myself into it, as I was reaching to belong to something. In the end, no matter what I did, no matter how hard I tried, they never accepted me *just as I was*. I felt outcast and alone. Even when I was there surrounded by people, in my spirit, in my being, I felt alone.

I tried hard, maybe too hard. I smiled on the outside, even though on the inside I thought I'd break into two. If I were being honest with myself, I really didn't like the church. I really didn't like the people. They had their church. They didn't want outsiders, and to them, that was what I was. If I had arrived on a spaceship and had an odd-shaped head and big eyes, I would have been no different than the person I was standing before them now: an invader. But with spaceship or not, I was an uninvited visitor from another planet. They didn't want me. I wasn't going to fit in.

At one point, I accepted it. It was okay. After all, I wasn't doing it for me. I was doing it so I could raise a godly family. I could manage it, but I was alone; you mess with my kids and I was an alien from a third kind. And then it happened, that spaceship landed. The final straw, one Sunday morning. I had arrived early as I taught a Sunday school class and needed to drop Trent off in the nursery. As I sat on the bench outside the nursery, another family arrived with their infant daughter. As they sat on the other bench outside the locked nursery doors while I was waiting for the caregivers to arrive, the worker showed up. She quickly grabbed up their pink bundle, stating, "Oh, aren't you just my favorite little one?"

I sat there alone on the bench holding my beautiful perfect tiny little boy, and I felt alone. I did not even look over there. I placed my perfect little boy in his pumpkin seat, went downstairs to my classroom, and taught the last Sunday school class with my kids at church. My beautiful little boy sitting there in that room with me.

It was the best lesson I ever taught. It was about Paul alone in the prison cell. I turned the lights off and asked the kids to think about sitting alone in that dark cell feeling abandoned, alone, forgotten, and betrayed. I couldn't help but cry. It was a bad day. Interestingly, a few of them cried too.

God couldn't have planned that lesson any better that very day. I left as easily as I arrived. It couldn't have been any less hurtful, any less painful. My spaceship descended into the clouds, and I vanished. I felt just like Paul. I, too, was abandoned once again, alone.

I turned in a four-week notice and drove to Sunday school class alone for the next month just to teach the class. Apostle Paul wrote to Timothy, "Always be steady, endure suffering, do the work of an evangelist, fulfill your ministry" (2 Timothy 4:5). I would fulfill my obligations; I was a bigger person. I never spoke to the pastor, the Sunday school superintendent, the pastor's wife, or a member ever again. Interestingly, none of them contacted me. I guess that after four years, it wasn't just a thought; I really didn't fit in. I really didn't matter to any of them in the end. I was alone again.

Sometime later, I did run into the pastor. I was waiting in a line to get some catalog items from JCPenney. He was standing in line and starting to argue with the clerk over a catalog and about how a person should not have to pay five dollars for one. In that moment, my heart smiled. He was arguing over a catalog. I had made the right decision.

In October of 2002, I wrote this:

I Am Alone

This is my life and the loneliness within it,
Stillness and quiet in a place where I can feel it,
Where I can hear it.
Ironic that among the midst the children keep me
Surrounded by sound, bustling them to programs and events,
Working tirelessly on their homework.
Still somewhere there is silence.
I listen with my subconscious, am I aware?
Or am I just sitting there waiting...wanting...it to be done.
During bath time, I put them in the tub...a moment...silence.
They play, and I escape to the kitchen. The floor a mess...the toys
I do not care. Silence, a few moments, I am feeling lucky.
Time for bed...relentless moments of last-minute stories,
Prayers, hugs, and kisses...then goodnight.
It is quiet...there is peace... I close my eyes, another day...
I am alone.

I was never really ever alone. Oh, sure, I felt like I was, but we know that God never sleeps. Right there as I lay cold and feeling alone, he was there with me. Although I was so broken, so lonely, I just couldn't realize it.

> I lift up my eyes to the mountains—where does my help come from? My help comes from the Lord, the Maker of heaven and earth. He will not let your foot slip—he who watches over you will not slumber; indeed, he who watches over Israel will neither slumber nor sleep. The Lord watches over you—the Lord is your shade at your right hand; the sun will not harm you by day, nor the moon by night. The Lord will keep you from all harm—he will watch over your life; the Lord will watch over your coming and going both now and forevermore. (Psalm 121)

My life over those years consisted of Play-Doh and coloring books. I kept everything neat and tidy, and all their toys were bagged, toted, filed, and sorted each night at bedtime. I think I was the only mom who knew how many Barbie outfits my daughter had or how many hot wheels would fit in each tote. I lived, I breathed my children.

Todd worked countless hours, and when he wasn't working, he was trying to get a few hours of sleep. I threw myself into motherhood, as it was all I had. Vernon Brewer wrote that "A great spiritual leader once wrote, 'God is too good to be unkind, and He is too wise to be mistaken. And when we cannot trace his hand, one must trust his heart.'" (Brewer, Vernon. *WHY? Answers to Weather the Storms of Life*. WH Press.) Still so broken, so defeated, so distraught, I allowed myself to be unable to see that God was with me all along. He had a plan for me, even if I couldn't see it.

Before the move, I had a few friends whom I was semiclose with. We made shopping dates and then early play dates when Justine was small. Once we moved, it was all on me. I was constantly loading all three of them up and making the "more than one and a half hour" trek to spend an afternoon with a girlfriend. The trips my friends made were getting less and less, and I felt more and more I was doing it all. Eventually I decided it was just too much work. I was better off just being alone and not having friends. I sent letters. I said my goodbyes and decided I was better off without them. Call it what it was. I was alone, even if this time I chose to be.

In the book *Depression: The Silent Shame* by Denise L. Shaw, the author wrote, "When we face circumstances beyond our control, the natural human tendency is to try and carry the load ourselves…when circumstances stretch us to the limit, we should be leaning upon the Lord…anything less opens the door to the enemy" (20). I was so vulnerable, and I had opened the door to Satan. I allowed him to walk right in my front door and into my world. I practically invited him to dinner weekly. I was suffering from depression and trying to manage it on my own. Without God, I'd say, "Satan, you can have me." Shaw went on to say, "Isolation is the most dangerous symptom of depression. Sufferers cut themselves off from everything and everyone, especially those who can help them the most" (Shaw, Denise L. Depression: The Silent Shame. Adoration Press.).

This trend continued. I didn't feel that our parents had much time for us either. There were no scheduled regular visits, no times that we could count on, and so we isolated further. My parents took vacations with my sister and her daughter. It made me sad that she got more time in one week than we got all year. I was constantly reminded that she was single and had no one. I felt that choosing to stay married made me even more judged, thinking if I was divorced, I would get more help. I felt I had no one.

I continued writing poetry to combat the isolation. One day at the McDonald's play land, I wrote this poem. It was August 2002.

McDonald's

I sit at McDonald's and eavesdrop on what people say, my children are off in the tunnels to play. From the table next to me I hear the children saying, "Please?" Their echoes to grandmas and grandpas don't seem to seize. Likewise, the children who have just returned from a week's trip to their grandparents in Louisville. Swimming, horseback riding, movies, and eating out. My thoughts drift back to the table beside me. I gaze out the windowsill.

They share a moment of happiness while mine is of fear. It is another lonely day. Another week and school start, the summer is over, what can I say?

I sit, I listen to this room filled with laughter. Each child celebrating a happily ever after.

I think of Lee who had court, Laura who lost her dog, my worries fade somewhere in the fog.

Again I see my example of fear. Oh wait, can it be? I touch my cheek, another fallen tear.

Why is it follows me? I can't escape it. This feeling is so deep inside me. Mixed parts of anger, frustration and fear.

What can I say? What do I do?

Their loss, their emptiness, I am alone.

It didn't take me too long to find another church. I knew I wanted to raise the kids in church, but after the incidents at the previous one, I had scars. I read something from an article that once said that scars were meant to heal and that the hurt was over. You had conquered the pain, learned a lesson, and moved forward. We began attending a large church, deciding that maybe picking a smaller one wasn't a great idea either. In the end, it also wasn't a great idea. Sometimes small wasn't that great, but sometimes big wasn't either.

Oh, we attended regularly and loved the preacher and the beautiful new church. It was a church out of a movie: a complete orchestra, each Sunday was a theatrical performance of epic proportions, the Word of God was preached, hymns of praise were sung, and more programs were available than the local YMCA. The problem was we were invisible. No matter how much a person tried or did, there was so much going on that unless you were part of the choir, the praise and worship team, someone on the front lines, not once but all the time you were invisible.

I tried to tell myself that, at least, I was worshipping God and that the people didn't matter. This was true to an extent, but I still wanted to have friends. I wanted to feel like I was a part of something. Needless to say, after four years, we ended up deciding that we wanted to move back closer to home. Leaving that church was like walking out of the mall. The only difference, at least, was that at the mall when you walked out your arms were full, leaving the church your arms were empty. No one ever knew you left.

We ended up buying what was, and is still to this day, my favorite home. It was a perfect little house—lots of space, beautiful on the inside, lovely. The problem was, it was nestled in a cove of other homes, let's see, I think it's called a neighborhood. When we purchased the house, we were told that the homes in this country-setting housing addition had been empty for years. Within one year of buying our home, more than six of them filled up. I guess they were all waiting on someone to make the first move.

We moved in on June 6, 2004. Justine was twelve, Grant was nine, and Trent was six. My dad helped us move, and we were excited to be close to the family, hoping that maybe with this move, we would alleviate the isolation that we were all feeling at this time. But that did not happen. Thirteen days after we moved in, my dad suffered a massive heart attack and passed away. He had just turned sixty-two on June 11. My dreams pinned to alleviate the isolation, and guess what? I lost the greatest man I'd ever known. Alone.

To make matters worse, the kids and I were at my parents' home. We were having an annual yard sale. It was supposed to be the perfect weekend. Dad and my brother-in-law, Tim, left to take all the grandkids on the pontoon boat. We were all going to meet up later for a cookout. Instead, less than hour into them leaving, the call came in—Dad was en route to the ER in an ambulance. His last words to us were, "See you later. We'll be back."

The kids, all of them, saw this. There was no escape. Scars, there were no scars. Open wounds were left gaping, bleeding. It was going to take a lot to heal them as my walk with God had taken a serious nosedive. My spirit, in addition to my heart, crushed. Rumi said, "A wound is the place where light enters you." I needed light. I needed something other than darkness, and we all did. Our children were changed, jaded. None of them would ever be the same. Another journey ahead.

Settling into the house was difficult. The move and the loss of Dad caused more changes. They were supposed to be good changes. Life was supposed to get better. What happened? Even though my search for a church was an ongoing dilemma, my walk with God was fair. Oh, I wasn't anywhere near being the next great evangelist. I wasn't anywhere near being the perfect Christian, but I did love God and I did work hard to be the best daughter I could be for him. If you want to test your faith lose someone unexpectedly *before their time*, see where that lands you.

That day in the hospital, I could remember it like it was yesterday. There in that waiting room, I was waiting for the doctors and nurses who tried feverishly to save my father. We all held, clenched tight fists, and prayed, "Please, God, don't take our dad." Then the doctor came in. He approached my mom with his head bowed. "He is gone." It was like watching a movie or dreaming a dream. Gone.

In that moment, like many moments before, it was as though the world lay silently still. All I could process was tomorrow was Father's Day and I don't have a father. I prayed to God to save my dad, and what did he do? He took him. I prayed, "Did you hear me?" I saw red. Not a soft hue of pink but red, blood red.

By June 24, 2004, when I was in my final class at SMWC, I dropped out, unable to sustain to concentrate on school. Heck, I could barely concentrate on living. My life was consumed with what-ifs and why nots. I lived with them day and night. There was no way of shutting them off. I remember that I was unable to go to sleep because sleep meant that he might get forgotten. I'd force myself to stay awake so I could remember. But remembering only caused me pain.

Sometime that summer, I was in the car with Grant. I asked Grant, as I had him and Trent so many times before, "What do you remember about Grandpa Jerry?"

Grant looked at me and said, "Mommy, what do you remember?"

I cannot tell you what I felt in that exact moment, but I know I was surprised.

For months, I spent so much time concentrating on the kids remembering their grandpa so they would never forget. I forgot that he was my dad. I wrote this one afternoon in my journal.

> *Anytime we talk about the past, we take a walk back in time.*
>
> *Our lives are built on memories we can never forget, those memories that helped shape who we are.*
>
> *We feel better knowing that our lives, their life had meaning; and through our memories, we never let it end.*
>
> *For me, I no longer have to ask my children anymore what they remember most about their grandpa. It matters most that I remember. It took that moment with my son to remind me that I didn't need his memories all along; I had my own. I don't need to rely on them to help me remember the past I have the power within myself to do just that. My dad left me his legacy: the tools to be the best parent I can be. From Ring Lardner, "The family you come from isn't as important as the family that you are going to have." I know my dad is proud of me for taking what he gave me and moving forward with it.*

Through the love of others, the previous encounter with Grant and the loss of Dad, the bitterness that enveloped me slowly began to fade. Oh, but my anger was still there. The seal that kept the envelope closed began to release its stronghold. Was I free? Of course not. Was I close? Of course, I was. But would I be? Not then. For once again, my journey would take me somewhere else, and from the words of Jerry Sittser, "One cannot win an argument with the almighty God."

Just along the road, within walking distance, was a country church. I was angry at God over taking my dad, especially after the move, as we wanted to be closer to family and then my dad was taken from us. I know that at this time, my heart was in the wrong the place, but I knew that without God, I'd never get through this.

We started attending this church, and I immediately signed up for a night class based on a Beth Moore series. I engrossed myself in the program and loved it all. I started to accept my dad's passing and *forgive* God for taking him. This was a bit fast forward, but Pastor Tim Moran gave a sermon one Sunday morning, and in it he said, "What is the one thing that will keep you from trusting God?" I didn't even have to think about it. The answer for me was simple: he didn't answer my prayer. Now I didn't mean the prayer that I came home and the house was miraculously clean or the one where my office was closed for some random unforeseen reason. I mean, a true mindful heartfelt prayer request. I put all my hopes, all my faith, and full trust only to have a failed answered prayer. Trust for me has always been "I have your back, and you have mine." When I need you, you are there. You lift me up, never let me fall. In Linda Shepherd's book, she said, "Effective prayer is not prayer that bosses God. It's something completely different. Effective prayer that trusts God no matter what." (Shepherd, Linda Evans. *When You Don't Know What to Pray*. Revell.).

The kids were quickly growing attached to the programs, and all three children were saved and baptized. But from the day of the baptism, a wheel turned, and it turned in the wrong direction. Growing up in the church, being saved, and baptized at the age of seven, I knew that salvation was received by the acceptance of Christ in one's heart and that it was by his blood that we are saved. This is how I was raised; this was my belief. As a Christian, we are all forgiving. We don't have to understand why some choose to believe the way they do, but we have to follow our faith, whatever that is, be it Catholic or Christian, be it by the water or by the blood.

That day in that church, during their baptism, the preacher said, "It is by this water you are saved." My oldest sister began crying, and the looks of shock on my families' faces were devastating. How could I have attended this church for more than six months and never know that they did not believe the way I did? What was wrong with me? Was it the grief of Dad that blinded me?

There were two weeks left in Beth Moore's program. I just wanted to complete the course. I knew in my heart that we would have to leave. There was no way to stay, no way at all. Just to let me complete the class was all I hoped for the night of the second last class. The series was wonderful. We had a good time of fellowship and a good time watching the video. This video was different, though. As it neared the end and the invitation on the screen was offered, Beth demonstrated Christ on the cross. Through pleading, she spoke about the shedding of his blood dripping from his wounds and that through this sacrifice we ask him in our hearts.

As I watched this amazing invitation of a godly woman, the TV was immediately shut off. Standing next to the screen was the pastor's wife who quickly stated, "Now you all know that we do not believe that the blood is the reason we have salvation, that it is by the water of baptism that we know our Savior."

My heart was beating, and my mind was screaming, "No!" I started shaking and looked at a fellow PTO mom who was also the one who invited us to attend this church.

"I have to go. I cannot stay, and my dad would be so disappointed in me."

She looked at me and said, "I'm not sure I've always agreed with that either."

I grabbed my belongings and bolted toward the door. Tears were streaming before I even reached the door. Lost, broken, invisible once again.

Without too much drama, I felt banned by the people of the church. Rumors were flying. I was snubbed. I even had a later run-in with the pastor's wife. There was a Bible verse that read, "Those persecuted in his name." I wasn't afraid. I was disappointed that this wonderful church was no longer mine. I was disappointed that I was considered the *wrongdoer*, the *outcast*. All I wanted was a place to belong to, all I wanted was a friend, all I wanted was to not be alone, and all I wanted was God. Paul was on trial *as the one who had caused a great fire*. Well, I didn't start a fire. I didn't even get a match. Contrary to others, one would have thought I had started a forest fire and burned a thousand acres in the forest. I could clock the church at 1.9 miles from home. I had walked it hundreds of times, making the loop around and back again; this was the longest 1.9. tears streaming.

I remember whispering as I drove away that last night, "Dad, I hope I made you proud. All I want to do is be like you."

Paul went on to say, "But see the believers of example in speech and conflict in love and in faith, in purity till I love—attend to the public reading of the scripture—to preaching, to teaching. That after times, some will descend from the faith and give their minds to subversive doctrines. Still, keep safe that which has been entrusted to you." Tears were streaming, hands were shaking, heartbroken. I knew I had done the right thing. I was alone.

However, the subtle voice of reason was in my ear. Persecuted, abandoned, defeated. It would take a while to feel renewed, to have the courage, the will, the strength to stand. There was a saying that said if you couldn't walk, then crawl…just get there.

> *Sometime later and through a work-related event, I ran into the pastor's wife, make that we shared a mutual case. She asked me to meet her in her office at her place of work, and I was terrified to do so but wasn't sure how to say there was a conflict either. After I arrived and sat in her office, it didn't take her long to bring that incident up. I told her that I was there about a case, not there to talk about something from the past. She wouldn't let it go; I had to walk out. I was angry yet again. I can't tell you how differently I prayed that night, but I did. I finally accepted that it really wasn't me. God answered my prayer. I was vindicated, and those who are persecuted in his name (me) found hope.*

The loss of Dad had left us hollow and empty. We felt alone and abandoned, isolated. This only brought the problems further. The telescope was on high; we were zoned in. Eventually no one was coping. Darkness had enveloped us all like a cloud of fog, and from Grant's words today, they were "like a pair of sunglasses in a sauna." All joking aside, there were many dark hours for all of us. I think in this time, I just gave up. My childhood in churchgoing was so picture-perfect in so many ways. I was a part of an amazing youth group I loved. I didn't ask to belong, but I was born into it. It was mine. I almost had a birthright to it, and everyone knew me. No one would believe that since we had moved back in 1993. I had been searching for another church to belong to, and it was now 2005. My search for a church was not over yet. I was alone.

In this time, I found a book written by Jerry Sittser. In it, he said the same thing I did. He prayed for safety for his family, and God did not answer his prayer. I had found someone who understood my pain. Through this book, I obtained more healing. Was I there? No. I was closer.

My sister, Lisa, and my brother-in-law, Tim, were attending a church and invited us to attend. I was really in no way ready to try again to believe in a church or a pastor, but we started attending. This time, there were scars, there were more wounds that needed light, and they were bleeding. I couldn't say that leaving their church was too painful. By now, it was like I was seriously not surprised. I didn't let it hurt, wouldn't let it hurt. No connections, no losses. This time, I was ready.

Another decision was right. The Bible said, "Come as you are" (Isaiah 55:1). No mercy extended to my daughter's friend who chose to wear a skirt too short for their liking. She was a child of God. She didn't go to church. After that, I don't know if she ever went back. We certainly didn't.

It was December 2005. Dad had been gone for a year and a half. I still had healing, spiritual healing. I knew that I longed for it, countless nights on bended knee, asking, "What do you want from me? How can I keep getting it so wrong?" Christmas was within a week, and I mustered the courage with Justine to try the local First Baptist Church in the town where I worked. We walked into the church and were greeted with smiling faces and warm embraces. The only regret I had was staying there. They offered little to no children's programs.

My hopes of raising the kids with the same supports I had wasn't going to happen. I did feel like I tried for this church too. I tried to participate to grow. In the end, it, too, just never felt like home.

I wrote this on March 2005.

> *Growing up in the church was I learned the lines. I convinced myself that I would play the part. The problem lies in, could I live the part? No more masks, no more color-changing skin, no more acting. This time, I looked in the mirror; it was going to be me...simply me. Inside my heart, the struggle was in the anger that was leading to adversity, the adversity to more anger, the anger to bitter confusion, and bitter confusion to that of indecision. I was in a position of indecision, and I had to find a way to make a decision. By pretense, we are sometimes pushed into a realm we cannot handle. We begin to let worries of the world control our every emotion, action, and feeling. Easy too, bitterness can take everything, and as it is, it is a lot of energy.*
>
> *Me simply me. Now I see, if I wear a mask, I can fool the world. Once while talking to someone, I said, "I can be a chameleon. I can blend into almost anything and into anyone." I learned to say what people wanted to hear, not what I really wanted to say. I learned to hear, to listen, to agree... I was a master at playing this part. Spirituality is easy for me.*

Did I write that? I must have been delusional. How in the world was it easy for me? A year and a half after losing my dad, Todd's dad developed abdominal pain. It was January 2006. Later he would be diagnosed with colon cancer and given a few years to live. He made it less than six months, and on August 5, 2006, we buried him. His battle was nothing like my dad's massive heart attack, much pain and suffering to be endured. All of us were beside ourselves. The loss of Dad had left us hollow and empty, and we felt alone and abandoned, isolated. This only brought the problems closer.

Next to my dad was my most wonderful, loving grandfather. I loved Todd's dad as much as any other man in my life. To this day, my heart yearned for his mentorship, his advice. Donnie Daugherty was not only the smartest man I ever knew but also the best advice giver. I distinctly remember his last few words to me before he became bedridden and was kept silent by his cancer. We sat on the edge of the truck bed. I had just given Todd his birthday gift a few weeks earlier. I was showing it to him. As if almost in a whisper, he said to me, "You have always been so nice to me." Choking with the tears that burned my eyes, I looked at him—so thin, so frail, so changed from the man that had sat before me many times before with laughter and a joke he had always ready to tell.

I whispered, "And you…have always been so nice to me."

He never spoke to me ever again. His death sleep came that evening. Losing both our dads fourteen months apart left us all in bad shape. Eventually, no one was coping. "Psychologically grief can cause all kinds of concerns with the chemical makeup of a person. Grief has caused animals to die, people to lose their minds, and spouses have grieved so much that their own life was extinguished" (50).

That same naive girl, who was still being naive, never realized that the sprout that surfaced for me all those years ago had found another garden. This time, the garden enveloped my children. They, too, left from suffering the monstrosities of poor mental health. Grant would later be diagnosed with ADHD and major depressive disorder, Justine with anxiety and panic disorder, and Trent with anxiety. Years of therapists, psychiatrists, medications, appointments, poor decision-making, probation, fees, court appearances, school meetings—face it, these events were life-changing. Some left scars, some left lasting impressions, and some left paths of destruction. A search for the peace—the peace I longed for, we all longed for. Years were spent on the silent cold floor while the silent tears fell; I needed to learn that kind of peace that came from God.

The next five years, our lives were a roller coaster. We moved to a new home in 2008 only to make another bad decision. The seller lied about the home, and we put more than twenty thousand dollars in it within the first year. Septic problems, flooded basement, and no water were ongoing issues. I spent hours using the Shop-Vac trying to save the carpet and countless nights without water, or in contrast too much. Covered in gray water and unable to shower, I lay on the floor under a fleece throw. I remember one night as those same silent tears that fell twenty years before continued to fall. I prayed to God to reach through the ceiling and through the blanket. "Hold my heart, God, hold my heart." If you've never heard the song "Hold my Heart" by Tenth Avenue North, listen to it. These words helped me sustain.

Todd worked the night shift. The responsibilities were on my own. I was alone. For years I had tried to help prevent suicides, and now I was the one who wanted to commit it. I wrote this on one of those nights:

May 25, 2014

If you see light, I see darkness,
If you see color, I see abyss,
Help me choose to see the light.
If you hear laughter and joy,
I hear silence, it seems to surround me.
Help me choose to hear the laughter.
If you feel the warmth around you,
I feel nothing but the cold.
Help me feel the heat so I can be warm.
If you feel your excitement of youth,
I feel nothing but the surfeit of old,
Help me restore my childhood and choose age is a number.
While you see your cup as half full,
I see mine as half empty.
Help me change my attitude and quench my thirst.
You see the joy, the opening, the beginning of a new day,

All I can see is darkness, closed before the sun even rises.
Help me see the expectancy of an opportunity and gain grace for past losses.
Just like night and day,
Sound and silence,
Heat and chill,
Dotage and decrepitude,
Optimism and pessimism,
A new beginning and end.
With your help, I can see the light and know I am not alone,
Help me gain the courage to be my best, it has never been a choice.

June 1, 2014

I pray God who takes this bitterness from me. It doesn't help me to be angry for the lack of sleep I receive. It only compounds the stress of having to do it all. This said, right now, I have no sanity to spare. Not even for the anger that in the end changed nothing. I will hope no one ever has to feel this loneliness. Again I spoke to mom. On this very day, she reminded me how much Laura needs her more. She doesn't have a husband, she has no one. I understood this conversation clearly. I am on my own again.

If I were a fish, I'd swim to the bottom of the ocean. I'd marvel at the bottom. I'd dwell in the coral, and if I would really be a fish, I'd choose to be the color sand so I could blend in, the one that others

cannot see. I'd stay hidden. How wonderful to truly be invisible. That is how I feel.

For the next five years, we were still riding the roller coaster. Grant did not like school, and school did not like him. He struggled, and the teachers did not care. They didn't try to understand his problems. All they saw was a defiant child. More involvement with probation, more legal fees, and more meetings. We tried to fight a system full of those who didn't care. We tried to advocate, but there were just too many injustices to face. Too many people were not willing to bend. I wanted. *We* all wanted to run and hide. We tried hard, but it seemed that the harder we tried, the worse it got. It seemed there was no rest, no end in sight.

Grant ended up in a juvenile center for twenty-one days. It was one of the saddest moments in my life. I worried constantly. My heart broke over and over. I lived in darkness. Pastor Shannon Benham told me to go through the home and said, "Rebuke the demons." I did this. I did this every day. Our family said our house was condemned, *damned*, if you will to give us nothing but bad luck.

At one point, Mom said to me, "All you can do is take it one day at a time."

I said to her, "Are you serious? I am taking it a minute at a time."

Getting Grant through his junior and senior years were tough. He did graduate, and midterm to boot. I think I went to school every day from August to December 2014. Countless hours of going up and down the stairs to get him up. My mom endured listening to me crying and venting. Her most common advice: "I think he just needs to drop out." My mom would tell me over and over that I was strong. I felt so weak. Dropping out was never an option. What I wanted, what I needed was to break free from it all. But that break never came. I felt like I was in hell on earth.

One teacher, Mrs. Shonda Klinger, was the only saving grace we had. We laughed, we cried, and I clung to her for hope, for peace. She held me up when I wanted to give in. She believed in Grant more than any teachers ever had in his school career. She saw potential when others saw avoidance, she saw frustration when others saw anger, and she saw a graduate while others saw a failure. I nominated her for several well-deserved awards, none of which she received. She was a teacher who deserved far more than I was ever able to return. If it had not been for her, Grant would not have graduated. Period.

In a devotional by Lysa TerKeurst, she said, "God, I don't love the situation, but I do love you. Therefore, I have everything I need to keep putting one foot in front of the other until I get to the other side." We did get to the other side, or so I thought.

Grant started college that summer, June 2014. High school wasn't a choice; college was. Things just had to get better for all of us, didn't they?

My journal writings increased. It was my refuge. I read and read and read, trying, searching for solace for answers. I felt alone. I needed people to surround me, to offer me hope, and to offer me a break, a day and a night off. That break still never came. I was isolated. Silenced. I willed myself to doze in every fiber of my being as I was praying. If stressed was a state of mind, I became numb to it.

Doubt consumed me. It seemed as if I had been praying for something all the time. A need was never fully sated, and one more was added before the darkness of the one completed. They just kept piling up. I feared my doubt for God to follow through would hinder him from hearing me. I needed a carrot, and at this point, I had taken the stem just to give me something like a mere fiber of a sweater, something tangible, so I can pull through another day.

In Luke 22, the Bible described that those who doubted Jesus, too, were even his most beloved disciples. Even in their moment of doubt, God brought them some of the most light. What about Judas who betrayed Jesus (47:48) or Peter who denied knowing Jesus (56:62)? Even Thomas doubted Jesus. Here we go again. I am not alone.

> I do believe but help me not to doubt.
> (Mark 9:22–24)

By January 15, 2015, more feelings of loneliness emanated from my journal. Doubt was still ever present. The heaven seemed silent to my tears.

It is the coldest hours that we become numb to all feelings. Hardened, frozen, paralyzed into a realm of silence. A last spoken word, a mere whisper from our quivering lips. Is this where God says, "I have your attention now. Let me lead"? I long to hear God as others say they have. I do feel his presence. It is like a soft wave that covers me like a soft blanket. It tells me, "Everything will be fine."

Tonight my heart is open. I am heavy with burdens. Please tell me my sins are forgiven and that my debt to you paid in full. Erase all doubt and fear and fill me with joy and happiness.

And whatever things you ask in prayer, believing, you will receive. (Mathew 21:22)

A month later, February 15, 2015, I made this:

I struggle every day to stay sane. Every night I pray for peace, for comfort. My body feels deprived. The stress has robbed me of my sanity and peace. I cannot sleep. Stressed beyond belief.

Grant was skipping class and sleeping in his car. His depression heightened to a level that kept us struggling every day. Constant worry, fear, racing thoughts, inability to concentrate—we were at the bottom. Each of us by now was fighting a battle. We each felt we were fighting our own battle, and each of us was feeling alone.

A few days later, I found Joel Osteen's book *Living Your Best Life Now*. This book focused on how if we think negatively, we will get negativity and that if we concentrate on positives, we reap positives. I gave everything I had. I opened my heart to the possibilities. I prayed with a newfound hope and desire. I needed a miracle to get through this never-ending trial, and I was hoping this new outlook was just the hope I needed.

My journal entry on March 22, 2015:

BREATHE

I cannot believe what I am forced to face. More problems, more secrets to keep. I am the keeper of all holds. No relief in sight, no reprieve. Hold on. I keep willing myself. Hold on.

My faith by now was going but not gone. Suitcases were packed, and I just needed the ticket. The ticket was out. I didn't think I could hold on for even one more second. I wanted to run to God as much as I wanted to run from him. This search for peace, for consolation, for hope, for rest, for air.

My commutes to work, my mind racing, every fiber praying, willing things, I whispered, "God, slow it down." I wanted to breathe just once without reminding myself to do so. I wanted to sleep without taking a Tylenol Pm. I wanted to pray at bedtime and not every second I could. I wanted, I needed a break—the break I had been longing for so, so long. I got my break if that was what you want to call it. If I thought I had problems before and breathing was something I needed to be reminded to do, I was about to have my breath taken away.

THE ACCIDENT

May 11, 2015

Another long day. Grant had been gone most of the day we hope at school. Do we know? No, we don't know anything at this point. Debating on driving up to Indy all day finally went by 5:00. We had no choice. I told Todd, "You either go with me, or I go alone." He chose to go with me. On the drive, I called the hospitals and police stations. We circled the school parking lot, his apartment, the local stores. No signs of the truck, and no sign of him. After several hours, we headed back home. I tried AT and T to see if they could locate him; his phone was off. We have been doing this for months. This shouldn't be a surprise or unusual, but something seems different. Something is wrong, Todd and I both feel it. We laid down and clasp our hands. I say to Todd, "Do you want to pray together?" He says, "I just did." I say, "Okay." Exhausted, consumed with fear we doze. My mind is saying, "Keep him safe, Lord. Don't leave him alone."

In May 12, 2015, around 6:00 a.m., the doorbell rang. Officer Mark Terrell was standing there. "Grant has been in a terrible accident. He is being airlifted right now, and you need to head to Indianapolis."

We thanked Mark, yelled downstairs to Trent, and headed to Indianapolis. En route sometime around seven thirty, Todd's phone rang. It was the surgeon, Jamie Coleman, MD, a trauma surgeon at IU Methodist who ultimately saved Grant's life. She told Todd that she was going to do the best she could do. He was in bad shape. Todd hung up and he told me and Trent what she said. I remember screaming, crying, and kicking the floor at that point. I knew it must be bad. Every time my foot hit the floorboard, I nailed my heart. That was where it was on the floor. I looked down and saw the center of the earth, darkness, abyss, fear so close to me. I looked out the window into the dark sky. A few stars still covered the darkness, and daylight would break soon. I made a wish that Grant would be spared. "The great world's alter stars that slope through darkness up to God," says Alfred Tennyson. I looked straight in the eye to my broken heart. There was nothing worse than knowing your child who was knocking on death's door, and you might as well be a million miles away. Dear friends, my heart wasn't broken. It wasn't cracked. It was shattered.

I didn't know how we made it to the hospital. Once there, we ran to find out where to go. It was horrible. People started arriving, the waiting room was filled up, and everyone asked questions. We had questions, too, but no answers.

At some point, Dr. Jamie J. Coleman, MD, came out. She took us to the consult room and filled us in. She began explaining his injuries: a broken pelvis, broken ribs, crushed diaphragm, damaged left kidney (later to have to be removed), lost spleen, damaged aorta, damaged colon and liver… I stopped listening for a minute, unable to process what part of his perfect little body was not broken. Racing thoughts…you can live without a spleen, you can live with one kidney, we have the same blood type, he can have one of mine…severe road rash. We didn't know anything about other broken bones or head injuries. We were in life-saving mode at this point. To make matters worse, his body temperature had dropped so low that they had to stop until they could raise it to finish. He was at 96 degrees and needed to be 98.6. Still left open from the surgeries, he was sent to the ICU under tons of warming blankets and blow-up warmers. I hugged Dr. Coleman and held her hands, I told her that she had angel's hands, and through my tears, I needed her to know that "Grant is a great kid."

We reentered the waiting area and filled everyone in. We were overwhelmed. Family everywhere. My heart was broken. A room was full of people, but I felt alone. It must have been 6:00 p.m. when he was losing so much blood that they had no choice but to take him back to surgery. Dr. Mark E. Falimirski, MD, was the one who did his next set of surgeries. He relayed that he reached around Grant's back to find there was a tear along his diaphragm that was bleeding. Cut now from each underarm from within an inch of his sternum. On each side just below his nipples, another cut was done from her sternum to belly button. There were forty-nine staples across his chest, but still his belly was open. I asked that Grant would be placed on the prayer chains. I reached out to public media; we needed a miracle. We had entered a hard season.

My first entry that morning was at 12:06 p.m.

> *Our dear sweet Grant Daugherty was in a terrible accident last night and life lined. He is out of surgery. He has lost a kidney, damaged his aorta and liver. His diaphragm is broken, cracked ribs, broken pelvis and lost his spleen. He is in ICU and awaiting another critical surgery within the next 48 hours. Presently drug-induced and on the ventilator. As far as the accident, we know very little as to what happened. All I can ask is that you stop right now and say a prayer for our beautiful son. I will post as I know more.*

That morning, Grant had a *trauma team*. This team would be with us during his stay at IU Health Methodist with Dr. Coleman, Dr. Skinner, Dr. Kays, Dr. Atkins, Dr. Borris, and Dr. Gaski. He had urology and ortho. His own pharmacist, Dr. Madison, was in charge of infectious control. On the morning of May 13, we were approached by Dr. Greg E. Gaski, MD, and Krista Brown, a clinical research coordinator, through the orthopedic trauma team at IU Methodist. They told us that Grant was a candidate for a program through the National Defense that Dr. Gaski was developing. This study utilized the blood of wounded patients who survived life-threatening injuries they were working on to save the lives of wounded soldiers, we said yes, if Grant's accident could help others to survive then yes, he could be a part of the study.

We were eventually able to piece together the events of the accident, although Grant remembered very little. Sometime around midnight, we knew that he swerved to miss a deer not more than a mile from the house. The truck was rolled several times. For more than four hours, he lay alone in the dark. We did not know if he was in the truck, pinned under it, thrown from it…it was really unclear. Obviously he was unconscious. He did remember wanting to get his phone. Around 4:00 a.m., a newspaper deliveryman saw the truck lying topside down in the middle of the road. He slammed into it. Both Dr. Coleman and the EMT, Tabetha Brewer believed that the severity of Grant's injuries were sustained during the second crash. All who believed that he had sustained them during the first one, he would not be alive today. The amount of blood loss was incomprehensible. That first night, the newspaper guy called Todd at the hospital, giving a few details. We never heard from him again. We did find out he was driving without insurance.

I was on my knees, and for a while, this was where I would stay.

May 15, 2015

> *"We are quick to give God the glory. He has been with Grant, and all of us every second… God is Good."*
> *Grant had gone back in surgery. He had to have a drain added to his pancreas.*
> *Although unable to recount the events of that night, Grant does maintain, "God was with me*

that night. I was not alone." He cannot explain it, no great out of body experience to write about. He just knows God did not leave him "alone."

We would be told numerous times over the coming weeks that Grant was an anomaly. The amount of injuries sustained should have led to his defeat, instead he survived.

Pastor Shannon Benham and his (now wife) Kellie came to see us often and on this day. Pastor Shannon, having endured his own health issues, knew how challenging the thirst that Grant had was. He shared Philippians with Grant about Philippians 4:13. "I can do all things through Christ who strengthens me." Grant clung to this verse. Many times a day after pastor Shannon had left, we said it over and over. Grant's lips mouthing the verse with the tubes protruding from it as the silent tears fell from his eyes. I'd pray at night, give him your cup, Lord, and quench his thirst as only you can. His thirst is far greater than I can imagine. I cannot make it subside, but you can.

Sometimes we don't like what has been poured into our cup. Remember Jesus in the garden of Gethsemane? When he saw the suffering that he was about to endure, he pleaded, "Father, if you are willing, take this cup from me, yet not my will but yours be done." (Luke 22:42)

The author went on to say that we either accept our portion or refuse it. Boy, we would all like to refuse this cup right now, we'd rather have it filled with Dr. Pepper or Mountain Dew, and I mean literally! We forget that a cup can hold more than liquid. Sometimes our cup needs to get through the dishwasher more than once. Sometimes it holds something warm, sometimes something cold, sometimes the answers to questions we never knew we had to begin with. But sometimes it's just God's way of saying, "It's your turn to have a drink." So we pick up our cup and we begin sipping because there is no way to refuse even if we are not thirsty.

After the guards arrived and Jesus knew he had been betrayed, he knew it was time to drink from his cup.

As I read a passage in Luke, I wanted to cry out, "Lord, you know you had a big cup and you wanted to relinquish yours too." And then I read on, "Jesus said, 'Peter, put your sword back. Shouldn't I drink from the cup the Father has given me?'" As I read this passage and study the passage in Ron Boehme's book, he said, "Peter was blinded by tears. It seems all was lost." I, too, felt all familiar sting of tears to my eyes. I was not putting my cup back in the cabinet. I know that I, too, just like Jesus, must drink from the cup that the Father has given me. Jesus accepted what God had given him with maturity and determination. His cup was the ultimate sacrifice. He didn't sip from his cup; instead Jesus fully consumed it. His cup was his life.

Sometime ago, I wrote about the circle of life, just how like the song went, "It takes us all in turn." No one is immune. When I face adversity, I look outward to others instead of inward. I said in my mind that everything for them looked like roses and here I was sitting in a garden of weeds. Then I saw someone else facing a challenging time, and I said to myself, "I'd rather have weeds in my garden than barren ground."

For each of us, life takes us on twists and turns. We move from one tragic moment to the next, one trial to the next. The circle, the wheel, just keeps on turning and turning. It's like a Ferris wheel, and most of us want off. We aren't at the carnival where we want the ride to never end. But notice I said we look outward and not inward.

After Grant's accident, people said a lot of things. Of course, there was the rumor mill. Couldn't have tragedy without that. People want to have a reason—a good reason—that something bad had happened to us. Of course, that made them immune. We all knew that this wasn't true. Then I heard, "Glad it is you and not me. Could I not do this?" What? And you think I want to? Remember my cup? I would just pour it out and ask to have it refilled with something better, something less bitter and painful. And this, too, not said to be hurtful in any way but said in a way that would give me honor for taking it in stride. Then "God gives his best soldiers the greatest fights." I didn't remember enlisting for the front line. I liked to sit on the back row—engaged when I liked, avoided when I can. I didn't remember wanting to stand in front. Again not said to cause me more harm but meant to give us praise.

In the end, none of this provided any solace; none of it really in the moment made any difference at all. I wasn't even able to wrap myself around any of it. My goal, my focus, was to get through each day. For Grant, to breathe is another day of life. At any given moment throughout Grant's journey, it was never about me. Despite the words meant to bring hope and comfort, unless they could make things better for Grant, the words seemed hopeless.

In the book of Ecclesiastes in chapter 5, Solomon wrote a passage that continued to be read at the time of someone's passing. More than a year and a half, as I continued to write our story, I found myself standing just yesterday while a young lady of nineteen was laid to rest. A funeral that no one should be attending. I stood in that cold tent on a seventeen-degree winter day. The pastor read, "A time to get and a time to lose; a time to keep and a time to give away." We heard it again and again. No one was immune.

May 16, 2015

> *The doctors tried to take Grant off the ventilator. I write, "To God be all glory, and may he have all honor and praise." Off the ventilator and one of five torso tubes out.*

We only had left briefly to grab a bite to eat. All of a sudden, my phone rang. and it was the fifth floor. Grant was off the vent and asking for his mom and dad, "Can you get up here?" We tossed our untouched food and flew toward the elevator. Grant chatted much this day about the accident, lack of memory thereof. His voice was raspy, and he was given some ice chips. He sat in the cardiac chair. The cardiac chair was a bed that would be laid flat. It would take a team of three nurses, as well as Todd or myself, to pull him across, holding onto the sheet that he was lying on. It needed a large amount of people to help due to the ventilator and all the tubes: the IV fluid, leg circulators, wound vacuums, and chest tubes. This process would take at least twenty minutes.

The equilibrium was painful, the pressure on his poor, frail, already-weight-losing body was disheartening. Fifteen minutes in and we were back in the process. Challenging for everyone. A bit fast forward but one afternoon, our wonderful family friend, Don Ennis, came to visit. Grant was going to be put in the cardiac chair. Don and I stood for five hours coaxing and prodding Grant to keep him in the chair. He was able to do it, but it was challenging. Once on the bed, they would then lift it to a sitting position with lots of pillows packed all around him. Once transferred, even under the meds, he continued in pain. He made a funny comment about the men in white coats, saying they were smart. Chuckling, we all said, "Yes, they are pretty smart." He asked where he was, and we said he was at the IU Methodist ICU, and he said, "They are the best."

His grammy said, "Yes, they are."

As he chatted more about the accident, he stated, "I waited a long time for someone to help me, but no one came." As the clock ticked, it became harder and harder for Grant to breathe. His dad made a comment about his scars. "It would be cool stories to tell."

And Grant said, "These aren't cool, Dad."

He slowly began to slouch, and almost falling forward, his lungs just gave out. He started to vomit, and within seconds, the room was full of doctors and nurses. His readings went from a ninety to a forty, and in seconds, that awful tube was back down his throat.

The sound of the machine began again, and where only seconds before I could see Grant's smile and hear his voice, he was lying flat with that horrible ghastly tube protruding from his lips. Each breath was reliant on this machine again.

They eventually sedated him as he fought it. Finally, he fell asleep. I was reminded in this moment that this was no sprint, this was a marathon. I closed my eyes and prayed silently. The background behind me was the echo of that machine. I was reminded that breathing was required to sustain life and that every breath Grant took was reliant on that echo.

Keep the prayers coming God is good. Due to the severity of his crushed diaphragm he was not able to sustain. He was re intubated within hours.

Little did we know that we still had almost 8 weeks ahead. This journey was not going to be a short one. Metaphorically speaking, Grant's lungs were opening about the depth of half a pop can, we needed the depth of a one-liter bottle. This wasn't going to be easy, Grant needed healing and to regain strength in his lungs.

In the book Proverbs for life (p. 10), it says, "Our patience is based on surface material, God sees straight to the heart." This was going to take time, God's time.

"Be completely humble and gentle: Be patient bearing one another in love" (Ephesians 4:2).

To give perspective to the picture of what Grant looked like, imagine if you can

Initially, two arterial lines with more than 5 drips connected.

Receiving blood transfusions.
Leg circulators.
Catheter.
Pancreas drain.
Five chest tubes including tubes and machines.
Ventilator (tube in his mouth)
Feeding tube in nose.
Stomach drain through nose (tied to the feeding tube)
Heart monitors.
Pulse meter.
Arm straps.
Blood pressure cuff.
Wound vacuums (2)

Neck brace.
Cooling sheets (his back left with severe road rash)
Straps tying his arms to the bed as he tried to remove the ventilator.
Even though it has been four days, Grant was still hooked up to everything we became grateful for the three miracles that we had already seen.

My post that day on May 17, 2015:

Grant needs prayer. Every chance you have, he is being so strong.
God is great, and Grant will get better…this process is just time.
For those who have not heard of the two miracles already, here they are.
The first that Grant had even survived and was doing as well as could be expected. The second amidst the injuries he has sustained, upon his arrival to Eskanazi hospital, the tear in his aorta of which they said as severe is the reason he was brought to Methodist. Then as I posted, once they went in to fix it, it was there but not to the extent they initially thought (e.g., no surgery). The miracle…that's the only injury that brought him here.
He is where he is supposed to be.
Another day but Grant is not alone.
High temps, unable to reduce vent volumes, dangerously low blood pressure stating it is likely due to pain meds.
If you're like me you follow a post for a little while, then you get involved in your own busy life and it becomes too much. Trust me I know how hectic life can be. But one prayer can change a life.

May 19, 2015

Seven days in. The medications to manage his BP are making him angry and delirious. Burning through them at a rate of thirty minutes, his metabolism is high. He had to be tied to the bed. He is angry, so very, very angry. It's hard to stay in there, hard to leave. He is so uncomfortable, so thirsty. His breathing is low at fifty-four, that of a COPD patient. Dr. Atkins and Dr. Kays told us Respiratory to start baking soda in his treatments. They will also start the pneumatic vest that will vibrate his lungs to break up the mucus. Grant hates it, it is painful, hooked up to everything else. His eyes tell us everything, he can't speak, can't move, he is afraid. Ten long minutes 6 times a day they come around to give breathing treatments. Oxygen should be at 8 he is at twelve. PT came in and said, "We've got to push him." Grant likes Jason. Tomorrow a feeding tube. (How many more tubes and where will they put them?) Pneumonia present, 103 temperature. Thank you for continued prayers. Please stop and say a prayer today for our sweet Grant Todd.

We did not know anything about his brain, head injuries, or whether he would remember us or not. All the scans showed no swelling or damage that they could see. Still we had to fear. (How could we not?) My mom bought Grant a dry-erase board, and he wrote "Popsicle" on it, spelling it correctly. He was unable to sit up due to the ventilator tube in his throat, and he could barely move his arm and hand due to the bandages, IVs, and straps. He scribbled "Tube Out," at least a hundred times a day. When we would say not yet, he would try a Hulk maneuver and shake the bed from side to side. He would get so angry and try to break his arms free. He would bite down the tube with his teeth and try to maneuver it out.

This went on daily. His irritability made it so hard to be in the room and yet so hard to leave. Nightmares, delirium, there were so many emotional and physical ailments that it was even hard to put them into words.

May 20, 2015

We are told today a possible blood clot from his lung. This is terrible news. They are doing a scan to see. The worst part is this scan uses dye to illuminate the lung cavity. The problem, those with one kidney should not have this done. We implore everyone to pray it is not a blood clot. He should be tracheid later.

In these moments when he Grant is having a terrible time he tries to escape the straps that hold him steady to the bed. He doesn't understand he is not supposed to pull on the tubes, he just wants them out. He pulls his legs up to bend at the knee, still strapped by his ankles, shaking his head and pulling on the intubated tube. His eyes full of fear. How many times must I run to the bathroom to cry silently in the stall? Days are so long. The more pain he has, the worse I feel.

Possible blood clot in his lungs. Scan around noon. Please PRAY *the doctors* DO NOT! *Trach around 3:00 today. The dyes that will be used are no good for a person with only one kidney. He is staying strong but needs all the prayers that you can give. Checking for CEDIF, trying to understand the 103 constant temperature. Pray without ceasing.*

"I have held many things in my hands and have lost them all, but whatever I placed in God's hands that I still possess." Martin Luther.

I miss Justine, I miss Trent, I miss Weston. Trent is trying to be strong and finish his sophomore year, Justine is trying to care for Weston.

> *Reality…the lawn, the mail, my dirty house…*
> *Todd says, "Don't worry about those things."*
> *Josh and Valerie offered to mow the lawn. Thank you.*

One day, my mother-in-law offered to clean my house. She cleaned one room and then left. I struggled between quick trips home to wipe things off and grab the trash. It was hard. Most days Todd and I spent from seven thirty to ten o'clock or six thirty to nine o'clock in the little ICU room with Grant. We shared one hard back chair with each of us having a butt cheek on it. It was cold, so cold, mostly because Grant ran a temperature and the nurses moved around so much they all stayed warm. We sat stressed and silent, cold. Each day we held on the promises they offered us. Time seemed to last forever, and yet in the same way, it stood still. Excessive worry, fear, tears. We clung to hope, to faith.

> Now faith is confidence in what we hope for and assurance about what we do not see. (Hebrews 11:1)

We would leave the room only to want to go back. We hated leaving the room at all. The first week, we stayed in the waiting room. We slept in uncomfortable chairs, we were cold, and we were nervous; it was rough. All through the night, another trauma patient was brought in. People were frantic making phone calls. There was no sleep. During the day there were no real place to visit family and friends. Many people gathered in the waiting areas. It seemed chaotic. All I wanted to do was to be with Grant.

Eventually, we began sleeping in the car. The waiting room was overtaken by the new families there. We needed to go home but just couldn't bear being that far away. The food was expensive, and the hours of the cafeteria were minimal.

Todd's brother, Jeremy, started a GoFundMe. The money from this website paid our bills while we were out of work, for gas, for groceries for Trent, for his lunch money, and for some nights at a hotel.

Through the churches, friends, family, Bear Run, and my work we ended up with enough.

Eventually, we went home to shower. We left around ten at night only to arrive back by seven; this included three hours round-trip driving. We did not want to miss those morning rounds. During one visit, Pastor Shannon and Pastor Tyra emptied their pockets, handing us all they had. Pastor Glover bought us food and drinks several times. Don Ennis bought some food and pizza. My sister, Lisa, and brother-in-law, Tim, gave us money several times, as did our aunt and uncle Nick and Phyllis Bowman and my mom. We knew they knew it was taking all we had to stay and to sustain.

> Faith produces favor, favor opens doors. Therefore, when we have a need for health, money, or anything else, our battle is to find a way to stand in faith with our shield lifted. *No matter what we need, if we activate our faith, every need will be met.* (Pierce, Chuck D., and Robert Heidler. *Restoring Your Shield of Faith.* Chosen Books.)

May 21, 2015

> *Terrible day. Doctors think it is either a bowel obstruction or the nonworking kidney. Grant is very thirsty, very irritated, and very uncomfortable. Doctors are deciding right now what to do.*
>
> *Please pray recovery is just around the corner...he is growing weary.*
>
> *"If we truly love people, we'll desire for them far more than it is within our power to give them, and this will lead us to prayer. Intercession is a way of loving others"* (Richard J. Foster).

May 22, 2015

Pastor Shannon stopped by and read scripture to Grant today. Grant was read his verse Philippians 4:13. Gratefully Grant is alive. Grateful I spent the whole day with him. I have helped him all day. Started Ativan and Zyprexa. Better day and all Praise be to God and may all glory, honor, and praise be given unto Him.

Things are better today, getting his long bed complete 180. Dr. Atkins said, "We still have one very sick boy here, but we will take progress."

Thank you to everyone who helped amp it up with me last night.

"Do not be anxious in anything but in everything by prayers and petition with thanksgiving, present your requests to God and the peace of God which transcends all understanding will guard your heart and your minds in Christ Jesus" (Philippians 6:7).

His arterial line was changed for the third time. They were running out of places to put it. Grant's anxiety was a daily battle. He pulled at the tubes and fought everything. They eventually started some Ativan today to calm him. They were not sure if the pain medications were making him delirious. Everything was a battle. Everything must work together, and yet it all worked against itself. One thing made another better, but side effects caused another issue. This then was pulled, and this was tried. The balance was troubling and challenging at best.

Three nights stay given to us by Pastor Tim Moran and his wife Amy. Tonight Todd left to go check on Trent. I am here alone. The hotel is one mile from the hospital with free shuttle.

As we left Grant at the hospital still drowsy from his third arterial line procedure, that sick feeling of him being alone left me heartbroken. Then as I watched Todd drive away I sit here alone. In ten days, the first time I have been completely alone.

I have continually asked that you pray for Grant and I will continue to do so. Tonight I ask for something more.

Hug your family tonight. Pray together and tell them that you love the, embrace this gift you have.

Tonight as my family is divided and my son is fighting hard, you have the opportunity to embrace health, safety and good fortune.

"To a great extent we find me must sow in tears before we can reap joy…you may expect a blessing in serving God if you are enabled to persevere under many discouragement" (Charles Spurgeon).

My God is an awesome God, and to my knees I bow.

May 23, 2015

Twenty-eight years ago today, Todd and I were about to say our "I dos." We sit in ICU with Grant. Bleeding still in his stomach tube, not uncommon as ulcers often form when someone hasn't eaten in so long. Using broad spectrum antibiotics to target it. Wanting to reduce the levels on the vent but still unable to do so. White cell count still elevated at 33,000. Pulled all ice, Grant's thirst is terrible. He looks at me and mouths for me to give him a drink when the nurse is not looking. If I do and he throws up she will know I gave in, I just can't. This is ter-

> rible… It so hard watching him want a drink and being unable to give it to him. He is angry, he pulls his legs up even though they are tied down, and he tries to pull his hands free twisting in agony. His eyes pleading with me to free him.
>
> He is cut from underarm to sternum on both sides with about half inch uncut in the middle. This was called thoracic.

In Hebrews 11:6, it said, "So you see, it is impossible to please God without faith. Anyone who wants to come to him must believe that there is a God and that He rewards those who sincerely seek him." I was seeking Lord for you to be here in these trying times; for you to reach through your sky; for you to take hold of each of us and embrace us in your love, in your safety net. Bring us through this trial where we proclaim a victory.

May 24, 2016

> Rough day today, new infection. Temperature up and no progress on the vent. ACCU was ghost town.
>
> "Therefore, I will be joyful always. I will pray continually. I will give thanks in all circumstances for this is your will for me through your son Jesus Christ" (1 Thessalonian 5:16–18).

This night, as we sat in the hotel room, I let go of my fear. I chose faith and that God would see us through. The test of more patience I needed to follow, but I would wait as long as it took.

> Wait for the Lord. Be strong and take heart and wait on the Lord. (Psalm 27:4)

I looked in a glass mirror but no reflection I saw. I was invisible. Imagine if you can a cylinder filling to the brim with stomach acid and blood, knowing that this comes from a large tube shoved down Grant's nose right next to the tube that protrudes from the same nostril. One tube was in place to put something in his empty belly, the other to suck it back out. Every so often bright red blood fills the tube and then the cylinder. This blood, from what the doctor said, were stomach ulcers from an empty belly that had been deprived of food for so long. It was terrifying, as they had to shift it.

Grant, unable to speak due to the ventilator tubing shoved down his throat and taped to his lips, grimaced in pain. I turned my head. My heart was hurt, the tears poured down. I left the room to cry silently again.

James Hinchcliffe was brought in to ICU fifth floor after wrecking during the Indianapolis 500. He was just down the hall from Grant.

May 25, 2015

> *Stop right now and pray for healing for Grant. They did not want to have to do the contract scan, but they will now have to do it. Five increments, one dose every thirty minutes. Temperature still 103, abdominal pain, high white cell 38,000 should be below 10,000. Dr. Skinner says that the fluid is either infected, surgery (exploratory needed).*
>
> *Grant will have surgery in the morning unless it is the Ileus. There is only a 25 percent chance they can close him up if they go back in, his body is just too swollen. This means skin graphs and at least six weeks added to his recovery time. Also while in there, they will remove the bad kidney. We need a miracle and the miracle is that it is the Ileus and that the obstruction clears. Start those prayer chains now.*

I cried this whole day. I gave up my fear and I thought the devil said to me, "I will bring it back." Maybe I didn't give up the fear. I didn't know. I could not stand watching Grant be so uncomfortable.

His pain made it so unbearable to watch. I am not sure if I cried because I was afraid as much as I just felt so bad for Grant. The suffering that he was enduring was incomprehensible. As a mother, I wanted to wrap him in my arms and make it go away. Why couldn't I this time? It would be a long night. Remember my story about Jerry Sittser, the loss of his family? What about Job who lost his family?

Horatio G. Spafford, the author of *It Is Well with My Soul*, lost his four-year-old son and then later his wife and daughters to a sunken ship in less than twelve minutes. Loss. So many families, so many men had come before us with loss. As I remember this story, I was in the middle of a storm. It was raging all around me, and all I could do was stand there and let it rage. I was not an anomaly. I was the same as everyone else. I would have struggles. It took tragedy and trauma for those who came before us to write songs, to have books written about them, to enter a realm of sharing and hope. It could take only minutes for one to lose it all, but all it could give was a lifetime of hope to others.

I'd made a reference several times about Paul and Silas. Even in their darkest hour, they sang at their loudest. Mountains and oceans seems like there's always another of one or the other... Its crossing your fingers when the map doesn't make sense, when the compass doesn't know truly north from truly lost: and it's up to you—you and your gut and your mettle, and your level of resilience, and your wealth and wisdom-to persevere, To get to the other side. (Sanders, Mark D., and Tia Sillers. *I Hope You Dance*. Thomas Nelson.)

> Wait for the Lord, be strong, take heart, and wait for the Lord. (Psalm 27:14)

> We can rejoice when we run into problems...they help us learn to be patient. And patience develops strength and character in us and helps us trust God more each time we use it until finally our faith is strong and steady. (Romans 5:3–4)

May 26, 2015

> *Our God is an awesome God, all praise honor and glory be given unto him. Dr. Coleman is not going in the stomach! They are calling in thoracic and he will likely have surgery on his right side to relieve the puss pocked that is causing the white cell elevation and the pain. Pray, pray, pray that he has a successful surgery and a good day.*
> *"I call on you Lord with I am distressed, and you answer me" (Psalm 120:1).*

We prayed, we asked, we implored, and he answered. We were blessed. In the book *When You Don't see His Plan*, the author wrote, "For a long time I sat there weighing human experience against grace. One you can accomplish on your own. The other you simply accept unconditionally with no checklist. Could I trust God with the journey ahead even if I could not see the map?" (Hennesey, Nadine, and Rebecca Baker. *When You Don't See His Plan*. Discovery House.)

May 27, 2015

> *Just met with the surgeons and infectious control. May be able to aspirate the lung abating surgery. Still running temps, still high white cell, still very, very uncomfortable. Plan is to jump start draining the fluid from Grant's right lung. Still on vent, still on broad spectrum antibiotics, Diagnosis today, malnutrition. What a blessed day. Friends' and family's prayer works. I hope that you can see that.*

Later that night, as Todd and I were resting in the truck, unable to get comfortable and sleep, I said I was going in to check on Grant. Todd went with me. Grant was in terrible pain, crying and alone. We immediately asked to see the doctor and get things rolling. The night doctor argued with us, and eventually we were able to get an X-ray upstairs. They said Grant's belly was so distended and they were not sure what was going on. They amped up his pain meds. I think we left from his room around 3:00 a.m. to retreat to the truck again after he was resting. At 7:00 a.m. for rounds, they said it was the ileus that caused him pain. He was given another injection to have a bowel movement. He looked like he was seven months pregnant. His legs were like little sticks sticking out from his belly.

We were on a roller coaster ride, and it seemed as though this ride would never end. Justine brought Weston into the room. Grant lost it. Both Uncle Grant and Uncle Trent loved their nephews. (At this time, we only had Weston. Now we had Cayson too.)

May 28, 2015

Fever is still up to a 103 today. They are ready to aspirate the lung to determine if it was the source of the infection, the temperature remains. Stomach is still so distended. Lots of pain. Testing our patience. Pray that it is the lung and can easily be drained. Thank you for all the prayers and support, God has this.

I began to read another book called *Why?* written by Vernon Brewer. He suffered a painful and debilitating tumor attached to his heart and lungs. Setbacks, frustrations, fears, and yet he remained faithful. His strength and perseverance remained unmeasured. For twelve days, I had feared the unknown, the what-ifs. He wrote as being told this by his good friend and mentor, Ed Dobson, "You can accept these circumstances from God. You know the circumstances don't make us who we are. Each of us faces our own circumstances, our own difficulties in coping with life and living the Christian life. Those circumstances do not make us what we are; they merely reveal the true character of who *we* are." Vernon said, "I knew what God was saying: accept what I am doing, wait on me. Be patient. Let me work in your life." (Brewer, Vernon. *WHY? Answers to Weather the Storms of Life*. WH Press.)

Throughout Grant's accident, several people told me that I had touched their lives throughout my posts and that through my faith, I gave them hope and renewal in Christ. Now this wasn't where I tooted my own horn or asked for praise for myself. It was where I said if you were experiencing hard times, others were watching how to respond to it. If you could demonstrate to others your faith, you could be a beacon to them in their dark times.

Pastor Tim Moran gave a sermon one Sunday about our response to adversity. I later found the story written by Alan Wong's restaurant. It was a metaphor that went like this: "An egg, a carrot, a coffee—all exposed to one element H2O and boiling if you will. How they go in to the boiling water is one way. The egg is fragile and yet returns hard. The carrot is hard but returns soft. The coffee, it actually gets better. The coffee becomes richer and flavorful. One element is exactly the same, but the responses are much different." I am not sure what we all went in to Grant's accident as, but what I do know is that we all came out like coffee. I'd said it many times, "We are changed, and we can never go back."

Through my posts, a friend wrote to me. It was on May 29. "I praise God for you. That the strength you show and the trust that you show inspires me daily. I love you and my family is still praying daily for Grant. May God give these doctors the knowledge they need to heal him fully in his name Jesus Christ Amen. Our God is all powerful" (Brandy Trivett). People were watching us, holding us accountable to our faith. If we wanted them to continue to pray and help us, we had to show them we could believe it too. That familiarity didn't ask from others what you were not willing to give yourself.

In Max Lucado's book, *No Se Trata De Mi* (*It's Not about Me*), he wrote, "Is there any chance, any possibility, that you have been selected to struggle for God's glory?" You cannot have a miracle without an impossibility. Faith, perseverance, trust—we were doing it all.

> For just as the heavens are higher than earth, so are my ways higher than your ways and my thoughts higher than your thoughts. (Isaiah 55:9)

May 29, 2015

Fever continues. Left leg is triple the size of the right. They did an ultrasound, no clots, not sure why. White cell count is down to 24,000 although at its highest has been 38,000. Cultures growing nothing. Please pray specifically that they find the source of the infection... He is quiet, mostly due to his high temperature. We are told he has neostigmine.
He takes the title HERO.

A *hero* is a person or main character of a literary work who, in the face of danger, combats adversity through impressive feats of ingenuity, bravery or strength, often sacrificing his or her own personal concerns for some greater good.

May 30, 2015

Malnourished, anemic, more pints of blood, by now I have lost count after 16, pain in his belly, still very distended, leg still swollen, so much so that it looks like it will burst, still on the IV drip for the Ileus. Another scan with contrast leaning towards a bowel obstruction or leakage. Puss pocket found on back that needs to be drained. Cultures from his lungs are still negative. Isolation status ordered again. We are in a battle among the scientists.
"The Lord, he is the one who goes before you. He will be with you. He will never leave you nor forsake you, do not fear and do not be dismayed" (Deuteronomy 31:8).
Pray for answers today, pray for healing, and pray for a miracle.

Oh, I remember this day—long, terrible. Isolation meant we had to use gloves, mask, and gown every time we left or entered his room. We were unable to hold his hand or rub his forehead. If I didn't already feel disconnected, this sealed the deal. I felt like he felt we were afraid of him. We looked like all the other faces coming in the room. I was not a doctor; I am his mother. I seriously hated this. It made me cry that we were treated as though we could harm him or he could harm us. He wasn't contagious. He had been getting antibiotics pumped in him for days. The antibiotics that were supposed to help him could harm him. This standstill was crippling we felt we were never going to leave. Tears. Many, many tears of desperation. The desire for patience.

Dr. Madison was on our side. He was the scientist with infectious control. He did not put on a gown; he treated Grant like he was. He said he would get to the bottom of it, and he did. Isolation pulled again. Thank you, Dr. Madison.

We breathe at 28 percent; he was at 50 percent. When they tried to reduce his ventilator settings, he just couldn't do it. There was a bad puss pocket on his back, and this would need drain to avoid more infection, as his back had chunks of flesh ripped from the gravel.

May 31, 2015

> *Preliminary reports: CT is clear. Dr. Skinner said that it is possible that the amount of trauma sustained is the culprit. It's hard to comprehend the amount of trauma sustained. He has a long road ahead of him and it is just going to take some time.*
>
> *We will ask God to help give Grant the strength and courage that he needs to push himself through and we pray the hiccups cease and healing occurs.*
>
> *Grant is breathing at 50%, when they even try 40% he cannot do it. We breathe at 28%. He is compared to a COPD patient. Right lung aspirated 5 cm of fluid, minimal. Also drained the puss pocket on his back.*

They started pulling some of the medications from Grant, and we were terrified that he would get an infection. The antibiotics kept him from getting sicker, didn't they? Come to find out they may have been what were the holdup. How many times in a sermon have we all heard these words "Leave it at the altar. Leave it at the door. Leave it at your pew. Leave it at the cross"? Vernon Brewer said, "When you lay your troubles and his feet, *you* can walk away with assurance that you have set the wheels of faith into motion." The wheels were moving. Grant was alive.

June 1, 2015

Temperature continues to be 103, counting breathing treatments and vent settings. Going to interventional radiology for another left chest tube.

Still debating on taking the kidney but will not be able to go through the belly and saying they will have to cut his back.

He's doing well despite the pain and they started 10ml in his feeding tube.

Consistently told me are in a marathon and not a sprint.

The vomiting has started…again. Aspiration is a constant fear. Pneumonia is a daily battle.

"I have learned to be content whatever the circumstances. I know what I need to know and know that I have plenty. I have learned the secret of being content in every situation, whether hungry, whether living in plenty, or in want. I can do anything through him who gives me strength" (Philippians 4:11–13).

Bottom Line: It's all about trusting God.

Please keep the prayer going up for Grant.

It's hard to express what this was like. I couldn't really even write it down. It was something that, in order to believe it or understand it, you would just have to be there.

Our faith was being tested beyond all measures. We were forced to believe in what we could not see was in front of us. We were forced to plunge straight into faith and believe without sight.

June 2, 2015

> *Left chest tube on hold.*
> *Plan is to remove the kidney later...*
> *He is sweating, his fever may be breaking.*
> *Please pray that God protects him all day today. Please start prayer chains.*
> *Surgery started at 1:00 and did not get done until 7:00 tonight. This was a long night. Grant's tired, weakened body forced to sustain yet another invasive surgery.*

I covered him in his prayer blanket, and the nurses kept taking it off. They told me the risk of germs was too great. I cried about this all the time. I folded it and laid it at his feet. I prayed that they don't take that comfort from me or Grant. I still smelled the faint odor of the oils, its aroma, like breathing in comfort. I had witnessed the ceremony of praying over the blankets in our church. I had watched them be anointed with oils and passed through the congregation. Holy they were. They were the *sight* we needed to keep our faith. Grant loved his blanket. Although he was unable to sit up and see it, he felt its warmth and knew that it was there.

Almost two years later, I had a dear friend's eleven-year-old son who was going through a terrible set of procedures. I called in a favor from my friend, Marilyn Walters. She drove it over to me so I could give it to a friend for her son. His mom, Kami, was grateful for it and said that it was a comfort to him. Knowing that it was blessed with prayers and held so much with love, they could be a source of light in so much darkness.

June 3, 2015

Sorry I did not post again yesterday. Initially Grant was to have a chest tube in at the left side at 12:30 and then the kidney out at 4:00. That all got changed and they took him back at 1:00 for the kidney. We did not find out until 10:00 they were taking the kidney out.

For the past three weeks, they have told us they were not going in through his stomach because his bowels were so angry.

At around 4 the initial reports from urology were that they went in his back, the way they told us all along. Then at 7:00 the trauma surgeon came out he had to be called in because they had a few spots on the colon tear, (because it was angry/swollen and was not to be bothered).

We were all upset because this was not communicated to us, a last-minute decision.

My mom Sue, my mother-in-law, Cheryl, my sister Lisa, and my brother-in-law Tim, along with Todd and myself, stayed in the waiting room until midnight when the lead surgeon Dr. Coleman called us.

I could only remember one day being distinctly angry at God, and this was the day. That day was June 2, 2015. They kept telling us that there was no way they could cut his belly open again. They had still not closed his vertical wound, and now they cut him on his left side near his belly button to just under his left underarm area to remove the kidney. Grant kept running high temps. His white cell count would not drop, and finally taking the kidney out was the only option left. I felt that taking the kidney was going to set us back even further, hurt Grant even more. I did not understand.

The surgery lasted six hours partly because in the process, they *nicked* the colon as we were told it was like a can of worms once they opened him. At around midnight, when Dr. Coleman called us, she explained that his diaphragm was attached now to his rib cage. In her surgery, she wanted to save his life, and the trauma was the only thing to do. She said that if they cut his back and opened the diaphragm, they would never get his back together again. I cried this whole day, probably as much as I did the first twenty-four hours. They were tears not of fear but of anger. Then after she called, it all made sense.

Each procedure for Grant meant more pain, more irritation to his already distended bowels. His belly was still open from the first surgery and now open on the side: cut open four times. The two belly incisions were attached to wound vacs. His stomach looked like a road map of a train off the tracks. The distension caused the wounds to look gaping when they would have to change the packing every three days. Constant pain, unable to get it managed due to his low blood pressure and delirium. It hurt to lie, to sit, to move, to breathe.

Feeding his empty colon five milliliters meant constant vomiting. Then they would pull all ice chips. Then they would try to feed him again. If he threw up, it was hard to watch. Tubes were everywhere. The vomit, coming up through the trach or around two tubes, shoved down his throat. The fear of aspiration was constant. Pneumonia was a daily battle. This had been a battle from day one. Even worse, after this breathing treatment, this was done every three hours around the clock; stirring up the mucus in his lungs made him cough it up. He was hungry, and he couldn't even get a tablespoon an hour.

I was choking, not on food but on tears. I didn't think Todd and I ate a meal without guilt for more than seven weeks. Remember my song from Tenth Avenue North "Hold My Heart"? It said, "How long must I wait, must I wait for you, how long, how long before you hear my cries?" For years, I had been living minutes at a time. This wasn't new to me. I knew I could do it, but the difference was that Grant's life was on the line. So much more at cost than before. The past was a fear of what *could* happen. This was living with what *did* happen.

My post finished that day like this:

> *We have been here since 7:00 and although they are working on getting a pain regiment going he able to mouth (still has trach) what he needs and holding our hands.*
>
> *In Romans 15:13, "May the God of hope fill you with joy and peace in believing, so that by the power of the Holy Spirit you may abound in hope."*
>
> *Our prayer: Dear Holy and Mighty Heavenly Father, creator of everything including this life we have. You control the stars, the sun, and the very breath we breathe. Throughout this process our hearts have remained heavy our fear ever present, our hope in the trust we have in you. We will do what we are led to do, continue to hold fast to our faith in you, and know that you are the ultimate physician. I once read where you "demand a victory in His name and accept nothing else." Our positive attitudes bring positive results. For everything you are to us, for everything you promise us, may we trust fully that you will bring Grant safely through this journey. In your most highest and exalted name. Amen.*
>
> *So blessed by each of you, we have all been supported by so many people, friends, family, and Grants friends. Remember Grant in prayer today.*

"When we look at circumstances we often look through them with the eyes of fear, instead of trust" (38). There was that pesky word again: trust. Was I still asking God to prove himself to me? I wasn't bold enough to challenge God, but if I wasn't trusting him, I had to question myself. Faith is the expectation that God is faithful. It expects that God will keep his promise. (Pierce, Chuck D., and Robert Heidler. *Restoring Your Shield of Faith*. Chosen Books.)

June 4, 2015

> *Today's plan is to manage the pain. Fever continues as does white cell count. We thought they were putting in another right chest tube but decided not to. Tomorrow… Nothing is growing in cultures so still questioning the infection.*
>
> *Today as I sat on the window ledge, "or the perch," as we called it. I prayed to have God speak to me. A young pharmacy girl stopped to ask if I was okay. I gave her the short story and she said to me, "If your son laid there for 4 hours alone and he has done all this, he will be okay." I hugged her and by the time we were done we were both crying. I told her she was an Angel sent from God to tell me that Grant was going to be okay.*
>
> *Please keep him in your prayers every day.*

Have you ever heard that voice in your head, the one that tells you to do this or that, to leave a building or stay? Was that voice of reason or the voice of God? Have you heard it and then turned away and later thought you wish she had done what you knew he wanted you to do? An opportunity handed to you to be someone better than you are to make a difference. Countless people walked by me that day, and yet she stopped to see what she could do. A mere stranger took my hand and held my heart and cried with me. Not more than a few minutes prior, I sat there asking God to send me a sign—my sign, my answer. I knew then what God, the almighty and powerful, was telling me, "Grant will be okay." No bandwagon, no sky full of angels, no trumpets, no massive parties on the ACCU floor, just a tiny humble beautiful young woman. Just like more than two thousand years ago, the night he sent the angel to share the good news in Luke 2:11, "Today in the town of David a Savior has been born to you. He is the Messiah, the Lord." My angel.

As for me, I hope there were more Brooklyn Mims in the world. I was glad she was a part of mine. A post later that day:

> *I just found out that the Angel that visited me went to Owen Valley High School too.*
> *If you don't believe God is working…well, he is!*
> *Praise, glory, and honor be unto Him. Prayers for a miracle tomorrow!*

On June 4, 2015, Dr. Rupple came in. He told me that Grant's right lung was full of fluid. They were going to try another aspiration, but it would likely require surgery. I was crying so hard that all I heard was surgery, another surgery. I looked at Dr. Rupple, and through tear-filled eyes, I said, "I have continued to stay strong throughout his whole process, but I'm getting to the point where I ask 'when do you stop poking and prodding?'"

That night, I couldn't wait to have my alone time with God. As I prayed in my heart, I thought of Abraham. His love was so great for God that he was willing to sacrifice his son, Isaac. Then in the final moment, God provided an escape. It came in a form of a ram.

I said, "Lord, I am not as strong as Abraham. I know that I am not ready to be like Abraham. I am not sure how many times I can say to Grant no more surgeries. Please provide an escape."

The next morning, they went in to do the aspiration. To our amazement, it was only a shadow and only removed a small amount of fluid. God provided my escape.

June 5, 2015

> *Surgery expected today for the right aspiration.*
> *Fever is 100. Starting belly feeds again to stimulate the angry bowels. My sister Laura posted this today.*

As I get up every morning, get ready for work…follow my daily routine, I can't help but have thoughts of this precious boy… He continues to face each and every day with a challenge but fights them one by one. He has such a strong soul and a heart that is bigger than life itself. I can't help but catch myself in prayer so many times a day I can't count. I just ask each and every one of my friends and family to continue the love and support (not to mention prayer) for my nephew. Don't ever take life family or friends for granted. You never know when an unexpected accident can change your life or the ones you love. I also ask that you pray for my sister and her husband during this tragic time, even my mother in fact. This is hard for everyone. We love you, Grant Daugherty. We pray that you catch a break soon and your body starts this healing process… God is good. We continue to rely on him. Each and every day.

June 6, 2015

Never give in! Never give in! Never, never, never, never. In anything great or small, large or petty" (Sir Winston Churchill).

White cell counted down to 25,000 from 30,000 yesterday. The average normal is *between four 4,500 and 10,000*, according to WebMD.

June 8, 2015

Dr. Ellender said they have searched everywhere for the bacteria and that they cannot find it.

Back to leaning toward the trauma and the severity therein telling us once again to be patient. Lowered the vent settings and told us that "he is driving the car." Since we have been here, this is the most progress Grant has made. Addressing his bowels today… hoping this alleviates some pain, helps him breathe and gets rid of the pressure. I have prayed for a miracle every day and I feel like we got one today.

"He is the one you praise, and he is your God who performs for you those great and awesome wonders you saw with your own eyes" (Deuteronomy 10:21).

So today on this roller coaster is a good one. Many thank yous and blessings to each of you.

June 9, 2015

When you are between a rock and a hard place, you can declare, "Lord you are my rock, my fortress, you are my God in whom I trust." And the angels of heaven will surround and protect you.

Saturday and Sunday were great days, today will be even better.

Removed 49 staples today, changing his wound vac for his two belly incisions. Holding his own, plan to remove some tubes today. He's going in the cardiac chair. Speech is supposed to teach him to swallow… this means juice (he's had nothing but ice chips for 27 days). We cannot wait to hear his voice too!!!!

Please keep those prayers going up, up, up! God has been so good to us. We love you and appreciate each and every call, text, and prayer.

> *Please also keep our other kiddos in your prayers. This has been hard on them too and our moms.*

> He that believeth on me as the scripture has said, out of his belly shall flow the rivers of living water. (John 7:38)

When living water was flowing out of your spirit, nothing would make you afraid. Nothing would stand in the way of your mandate to pursue, to overtake, and to recover it all. Another day. It was day 28. He still had a high white cell count. All antibiotics were discharged again. Time would tell. Three shots today for a person living without a spleen. They took his catheter out and down to one chest tube and another drain. Wound vac was off, and now just the moisture packed the belly incisions, still reducing vent settings. Taking time, the ileus was still distending his stomach, and deep breathing was difficult… doing phase conditioning. Pain related to the ileus, pain medications make it worse. It was a vicious cycle. I had this sickening fear that he would want pain meds for life, that he would be an addict to opiates, and that he would never be a *normal* kid again. The amount of meds was incomprehensible to me at this time.

Todd and I checked out an LTAC today. Expected to stay there for twenty to thirty days. We continued to ask you to pray as we transitioned into a new phase. The work for Grant would only get harder. (Is that possible?)

June 10, 2015

> *"The Lord will fight for you, you need only to remain still" (Exodus 14:14). I just finished another book entitled, "He Came First." It's an amazing book about being a breaker for God. Meaning breaking past being the average Christian. Near the end it talks about how God backs us against a wall*

so we lean on his arm. So we breathe and we hear God speak, "Stay calm, I am here."

We did not know if Grant was a boy or a girl that day in the delivery room. It wasn't until we heard his first cry and the Dr. said, "You have a son."

Today speech came in and ever so carefully removed the cover to his trach and replaced it with a speaking valve. She asked if he wanted to say anything, and he said, "Hi mom." Although muffled by the sound of the tube it was like his first cry. I bowed my head and said, "thank you Lord, I have my son."

She also gave him some orange juice.

As the nurse removed the wound vac material, it tore some arteries. The blood began squirting, and the tears started flowing. Not only did this hurt Grant, but the sight of the blood sent him into a panic. It was terrible. They called in trauma who had to give him shots and then stitches to repair the damage. As I watched the trauma surgeon sew the stitches, I looked at the wound that was gaping, and I saw inside the bleeding flesh. Grant kept wanting the bloody sheets removed, but they couldn't do anything until he was stitched up. As I held tightly to his hand, the tears just fell. He could not speak, and all he could do was cry.

Later they brought a drink for his liquid trials. He asked for a Mountain Dew. They only had diet, but he wrote, "That tastes good." It was his reward for being so brave.

June 11, 2015

"Nothing is more effective that a deep, slow, inhale and release for surrendering what you can't control and focusing again on what is right in front of you." Oprah Winfrey

Today was emotional as we said goodbye to the awesome trauma department and providers at the ACCU unit, 30 days in ICU.

Methodist hospital holds the elite of the elite. Every doctor, RN, RT, PT, and the list went on, were professional and top-notch. It's hard to simply say thank you for what they all have given us.

Dr. Coleman came in to tell us goodbye and we were all crying. Again, it's hard to simply say thank you.

I shared with Todd a quote today from Schindler's List "Whoever saves one life, saves the world entire."

We just arrived at Kindred Hospital. Here they will work to get rid of the ventilator, NG tube and feeding tube. Lots of PT.

As we thank everyone at IU, we thank you as well. The out pouring of strength, wisdom, and support and love have helped each of us endure. Messages have been like a beacon on these long, dark nights.

I close tonight by saying, the very first time I met Dr. Coleman I told her I needed her to know that Grant was a great kid.

Today through tears she told Grant, "Your mom told me that very first night you were a great kid… I know now, you are. God has a higher purpose for you, go fulfill it."

Last night at kindred was scary for all of us. He began vomiting right after we got there many times. It was more like one great room where all the patients were there together, separated by only a cloth partition at best. Next to Grant was an elderly lady strapped to her bed. She groaned and pulled on her bed, trying to release the straps that held her. This frightened Grant. Unable to speak or to move due to the ventilator, all he could do was stare and show so much fear. I told him that I would stay with him if he wanted. He said that I could leave. These were the nights we needed the money to stay in the hotel. There was actually one within walking distance to the LTAC.

Todd and I stayed there this night to be close if they called us. We were back over there by 7:00 a.m. Grant was terrified. He cried and threw up constantly. Finally, after pleading with them, the staff realized that this was very anxiety-provoking. Grant was moved to a private room after his first night in the ICU room.

June 12, 2016

Today was much better, today was actually great.

Grant began crying. He mouthed around the protruding tubes, "I'm tired of being sick." We said, the rest is up to you, work hard, do your best. To this he says, "I got this." Yes, fellow prayer warriors, we got this!

Pray we are out of here soon. We serve an awesome God.

June 13, 2015

"Patience and perseverance have a magical effect before which difficulties disappear and obstacles vanish" (John Quincy Adams).

Since our move to Kindred, it has been rocky, constant sedation what seems like over medicated, minimal PT, and constant vomiting.

Since they moved him late Thursday and then with the weekend, we have been told that things move slow. We are hoping it gets moving in all areas tomorrow so he can get home soon!

Please pray that tomorrow things begin to look up. Sometimes the non-movement is the hardest.

"Be calm and take hear, wait for the LORD*"* (Psalm 27:14). *We continued to say thank you.*

"What peace is ours when we realize that God himself has promised to carry the responsibility for our children! They were his before they became ours. He will be their teacher. He will establish them in righteousness and peace" (Paula Rinehart).

June 14, 2015

I've started another book… I know that prior to this happening to Grant I read people prayer requests, stopped what I was doing, really did think of them often and used Facebook as a vice to strengthen my prayers for others.
I also did something else.
I found myself silently closing those prayers with "Thank you, that it isn't me."
Almost willing it with my thoughts to keep it from me. I realize now that isn't a one of that is invincible of tragedy.
When you sit in a waiting room off and on for 5 weeks you build friendships with people you might have otherwise not (a chance meeting). The only thing that brought you together was tragedy. Dr. Rupple told me, "that is the thing about trauma, one day life is good, the next everything you knew is completely changed." We have exchanged hugs, tears, and numbers and become Facebook friends. We have rejoiced when someone went home and held hearts when some didn't.
My eyes have been opened to a world I never knew existed, if I did, it was only in my dreams, the really bad ones.

We are still at the LTAC, things are moving slowly. Grant has a pocket of fluid on his right lung. They have started Lasik's to see if that helps, if it doesn't he will have another aspiration. Holds up getting off the vent. Bowels still an issue, pain still and issue. I told the NP today I feel like we are on a hamster wheel, I want off. Imagine if you can how much Grant does.

"Consider it a sheer gift friends when tests and challenges come at you from all sides. You know that under pressure your faith life is forced into the open and shows its true colors. So don't try to get out of anything prematurely. Let it do its work so you become mature and well developed not deficient in any way" (James 1:2–4).

So please continue to pray. We stay calm, we gain patience to sustain.

"In life, patience is about waiting. It's the ability to keep a good attitude while working hard on your dreams, knowing it will be worth it." So if you're going to try, be willing to go all the way. And I love this part of the passage: "It could mean not eating or sleeping where you are used to." (Marc Chernoff. *8 Things to Remember When Everything Goes Wrong*. Accessed 2015. http://www.marcandangel.com/2014/01/08/8-things-to-remember-when-everything-goes-wrong/)

Patience was an ongoing need. Its practice was one of the hardest tests for us. Remember when I wrote "Slow it down"? I think God was still saying you were not getting it. Eventually you would.

Our first night at Methodist, we met Alice Book. Her husband, Paul, was in ICU as well. Paul had been there about a week once we arrived. We slept the first week in reclining chairs with Alice and her sister. We shared stories, laughter, frustrations, and tears. We clung together for hope and reassurance.

When we weren't in the rooms with our boys, we sat in the waiting room watching the clock or listening to other people's conversations. At night, we would sneak into the bathroom to wash our faces and brush our teeth. No places to keep our belongings; we kept them inside bags often unattended.

The waiting rooms were so crowded that our sleep chairs were often filled throughout the day with strangers, only to become vacant after 7:00 p.m. when you had to request a special permission sticker for after 7:00 p.m. We also met another family, the Sieber family. Scott had been in a motorcycle accident, and we met his brother, Mike, and wife, Rosemary. We talked, we cried, we prayed that after the surgery, they would both be okay.

Finally, we met another friend, Dana Dobbs. I remember the night that Ted was brought in. It had been a long night, and Dana was terrified. Frantically she made calls to her family throughout the early morning hours. We kept trying to put to rest the worries of the day, if only for a while. Dana was experiencing what we had, that first night of many long ones. As I wrote this, we all stayed in touch. Paul and Scott did not survive their injuries. Ted continued to recover. The day Scott passed away was the day Grant's kidney was removed. It was a long day, and we did not know Scott had passed away until Grant returned to the ACCU floor.

A week after the funeral, Mike and Rosemary returned to see us. So good to see them again but so heartbroken for the loss of Mike's brother. It still made me cry to think of them. What a fighting family they were. I stayed in touch through social media with Dana, Alice, and Rosemary.

June 16, 2015

Today I went home alone for the first time in more than 4 weeks. I played with Weston and spent time with Justine and Trent. Todd stayed the whole day by himself with Grant.

Yesterday was rough, I have been calm and polite and still yesterday, but I did exercise my advocacy and today the ball was rolling, really rolling.

Grant was in the cardiac chair, PT came in several times he stood up and they have reduced his pain meds. Todd said it was a busy but great day. If progress keeps up things will hopefully move quick. Grant is a rock star.

We had several visitors and then after everyone left I looked out the window and saw a cardinal. Grant's grandpa (Jerry) loved cardinals. I can't see one that it doesn't cross my mind. Interestingly as well I read this passage written by Victoria McGovern, "May you come to find comfort in and remember that cardinals appear when angels are near. So go now, sit outside and drink your tea, keep look out for the little red bird- it is there, it is where your loved one will be."

Todd and I got tired of the expensive, gross, cafeteria food. One day we ventured out on a walk and found a Hardees a few blocks from the hospital. One day while sitting outside at one of the tables a sparrow landed. I started tossing tiny bites and it quickly ate them up. On the walk back Todd started humming," His eye is on the sparrow."

Tonight I was thinking about this song and even more so after the cardinal.

The song was written by Mrs. Dolittle. Bedridden for more than twenty years, she said, "His eye is on the sparrow, and I know he watches me. "She never complained she praised God all the same. The song was written because of she and her husband who despite her being constrained to the bed they remained happy Christians.

Then I remembered a quote on Grant's Facebook page he was inspired one night after watching GI Jane.

> *"I never saw a wild thing sorry for itself. A bird will fall frozen, dead from the bough without ever having felt sorry for itself"* (D. H. Lawrence).
> God made the birds, God made Grant, God is good, and God bless you all.

These short home stays my heart was torn between wanting to continue to be at the hospital and yet be where my other children were and my grandson. My heart so divided I did not know what I was supposed to do. Guilt emanated from me. I wasn't cooking, I hadn't been there as Trent wrapped up his sophomore year. I felt that Trenton was on his own and in a lot of ways he was. We had to trust that he was making good choices and had food to eat (leaving money on the counter between early morning hours trips home to shower). A bit fast forward but this impacted him a lot. I think he felt that he was not loved as much and felt left behind. This just was not true. Todd and I were trying so hard to get it right, how could we be getting it so wrong? The only way I think I can explain it to Trent is be a parent and then you will have your answer. Trenton had come to the hospital about three times, I have lived it for 56 days. I am the one who dried every tear, witnessed every battle, I had to hear the words over and over and over, "we don't know." You go where you are needed, you go where your heart tells you. If Grant has not survived his injuries, I would have not wanted him to go alone. I would have wanted to have been there, I would still have a lifetime to share with Trent. I hope that he understands that, Justine too. It was never a choice, in that moment the choice was taken from me. This didn't help much getting him through his junior year. It was like living through it with Grant all over again. Trent wanted to drop out and give up. I think part of this was residual from the accident, part of it him still trying to make his mark on life and find his way. He fought me every step of the way. I felt like he hated me. He should have known by now that I never gave up on his brother and I would never give up on him. Interestingly Trenton is very smart and so very capable. Trenton's battles weren't academic but emotional. I felt myself doing the same things almost if you will in a sense robotic. Trusting that he would have that same fight in himself. I had taken Trent to get some medications, some help but he was so angry and determined he could battle it alone (sounds like his momma here) that he could do it...and he did. Trenton stayed the course and graduated and it was a wonderful, grateful, happy day. His graduation was far more than anyone may have realized, it was ground breaking for him. I was grateful for those who took time to celebrate this day with him. He had to have fight and determination and his strength in that year was monumental. For Trenton the sky is the limit and I hope he never stops reaching for it.

This very same day, my sister, Lisa Ferree, posted this:

So thankful for answered prayers. For the prayers for family, friends, and people we don't even know who have prayed for my nephew Grant through his recent accident and day to say struggle just to survive. We give God all glory, honor, and praise for the work he has done in the life of Grant and the love of family and friends that have been touched somehow through his trial. We tend to take things for granted in our busty day to day activities and focus on ourselves and rely on our own strength. We think to ourselves, hey, I'm doing pretty good here on my own and take the focus off our creator who made us and desires to have our full attention on him. When trials come into our lives, we have no choice but to stop and focus on the trial and stop looking at ourselves. This hopefully in turn brings us back around to God. And then we rely on His power and strength and not our own. As the book of James reminds us Count it all joy when the trials come up on you for trying our faith worked patience. This time during Grant's fight for his life patience has sure been needed. Thanks to each person who may have not even seen or heard, but while reading or hearing has taken a moment to stop and take the focus off themselves and look to God and ask a special prayer for Grant. I challenge you today, to stop and look to God, thank him for what you have, for who he is, and tell him you love him. Please continue to pray for Grant.

June 17, 2015

One week ago today, we arrived at Kindred. The adjustment for all of us has been just that. We were carefully warned by the RNs at Methodist.

Countless times at the ACCU floor we would hear the words "Code Blue." This was about as common as the nursery rhyme they played each time a newborn entered this world.

I became immune to it: the sounds, the buzzes, the beeps, the sound of the ventilator, slamming doors, pointless conversations in the hallway, laughter. (Seriously, who was laughing?)

Yesterday I lost my immunity.

I had spent the night here as Grant was not adjusting to being at Kindred. Todd and I had been able to stay a few nights at the hotel to be close to him; however, money by now had run out again. Since he was at Kindred, still on the vent but doing better we felt a little safer going home at night. We were home at least 6 to 8 hours to shower and change clothes. This night however, Grant did not want to be alone, I said I'd stay. Todd arrived later that afternoon. Grant had just been to physical therapy and they were getting him back into the bed. Todd and I said we were walking down to the hallway chairs to talk a minute and we would be right back. We left Grant's room for less than 10 minutes and in that time we here "RT to room 107, Code Blue," over the loud speaker.

Let that sink in.

Terrified we ran down the hall following every other nurse racing ahead of us. We can see them "bagging" Grant. We stood outside the room, tears streaming.

For the first time, "Code Blue 107" stopped me. I was frozen, my immunity stripped I stood there, code blue meant something more.

I got chills writing that, reading it again. Grant ended up being fine. His blood pressure had bottomed out, and he passed out once they had him lying flat. The ventilator noticed a shift in his breathing, and the alarms were sounded. I had been there all night, barely slept. I had no shower and now had one of the worst scares since this whole process.

For five weeks, we had watched our son tether on life and death. Today we thought he did. For weeks, Todd and I had exercised a level of selflessness. Our character humbled, our knees constantly bent.

Today has been better. He is still on the vent/trach. He has pneumonia again on the right lung, but things are looking better. He's actually asking for some food and drank a Sprite. Grant has remained so very strong and has not complained one time. He stays motivated to get better, very polite to the providers, and smiles when family visits.

Today when you are faced with hiccups pray for Grant. Is what you are facing all that bad?

"Remember, God has told us that we live in a world that will always have imperfections. But he is bigger that the negative and wants you to still enjoy all the good that is here. Grasp his hand and do what he does. He stays involved and is able to bring good out of everything negative."

June 19, 2015

> *You cannot have a miracle without an impossibility. God gave me the peace and assurance that he is not finished with my life and he has the power to accomplish his purpose.*
>
> *We are sitting in Grant's room. We are watching TV. As I sit here, Grant can't talk. We just sit together.*

Grant had either the intubation tube or the trach tube in his throat or in his mouth since we had been here. Grant was never able to speak during these times; his voice box was closed off. All he could do was write on his dry-erase board. We could only sit in silence. I watched his eyes, and although he didn't do much when I was there, I knew that my presence was what he needed. I knew he must feel alone just sitting there. What a journey this had been for him. I considered a part-time return to work and then thought there was no way I could try to help others, knowing my son was lying in this bed alone.

> *He is eating some fruit and sitting in his wheelchair, motivated to get better, they started the CPAP. Although slow progress was made. Each day we all hope we get him closer and closer to getting off the ventilator. I think we are all just waiting for this day.*
>
> *Sometimes it seems time stands still. We just sit and wait for what seems like forever. Each day we walk in here I say to myself, today, we will have a miracle.*
>
> *After deputy Terrell knocked on our door at 6:00 a.m. on May 12, it seems we have been waiting and waiting and waiting, for surgery, blood work, results, the Dr. to get rid of this tube, that tube, this or that, to go home.*

It's frustrating being a slave to waiting.

Then today I realize something. We were given a miracle the day Grant was born; we were given a miracle that Grant is alive. I have been waiting on a miracle I already have.

Please continue to pray for patience for all of us. Again overwhelmed by the continued prayers, love, and support, blessed.

June 22, 2015

"Father I'm bringing you my trials and my frustrations. You know each and every detail. Please comfort me as only you can, provide exactly what I need for today" (Our Daily Bread, June 22, 2015).

I think throughout this whole process we have felt every emotion: today, anger. We have been waiting days for Grant to get those nose tubes out. The doctor came in ready to take them out, and Grant says, "leave them in." What? Are you serious? Totally frustrated, I left the room (not before grabbing my current read), unable if you will to understand.

Justine and Trent came up to visit today. It was great to see Weston Lee and for them to see their brother. I didn't' realize it but my cup was empty, drained, nothing left but a faded froth line. I needed it filled again…filled with something besides fluorescent lighting, beeps, and pressure sounds.

In Ephesians 6:13–16, "He gave us a belt of truth, armor of righteousness, shoes of peace, a hat of salvation, the shield of faith, the sword of the Spirit which is the word of God and the power of prayer. "This whole winning wardrobe and nothing to *cover our backside, why? Because we don't run from out problems. He gave us the armor to face anything and everything head on" (135).*

So I put on my big girl panties, marched in there, found the dietician and we start protein shakes and protein shots tomorrow. These tubes will be gone if I have anything to say about it.

God has been so good to us. He allowed our son to live and continues to place in front of us everything we need.

CPAP continues, hopefully soon those pesky tubes out, PT continues. Progress is slow but any movement is movement. Pray that Grant is able to adjust to the transitions. Pray he continues to get strong.

"Be strong and very courageous..." (Joshua 1:7).

Our continuous thank you for everything.

June 24, 2015

"I run with purpose in every step" (1 Corinthians 9:19–27).

Today Grant walked the hallway and made it forty-five minutes with the speaking valve and trach collar and was allowed to sit outside for ten minutes.

We have been told it will still be awhile, he will need to get to twenty-four hours on the trach collar. He is getting stronger but still very weak. I said those tubes would come out and they did! Make that he removed them!

All in all, things are moving, slow albeit, but that's okay.

"Long is not forever" (German Proverb).

On this day, I posted a picture of Grant and me outside.

> *Reassurance through faith, blessed by the support of each of you, embraced by your kindness, enveloped in your prayers. "Our good friends and fellow Hot Rod buddies Bill and Carol Miller were wonderful to us. They came and visited with us several times and were true prayer warriors. She told us to remember Joshua 1:9. "Have I not commanded you? Be strong and courageous. Do not be afraid; do not be discouraged, for the* LORD *your God will be with you wherever you go."*

By now, money for us was low—make that *nonexistent*. Neither Todd nor I had worked since that day in May. Gas, groceries for home, Trent's lunch money, the parched barrel—our GoFundMe brought us just over $2,500, which was already depleted. Throughout the process, it seemed trivial to think of, but at the same time, it was reality. The bills were piling up, and we didn't know what to do. We continued to trust and pray and hope that God would see us through. He hadn't left us yet.

June 27, 2015

> *"There is no greater love than he that would lay down one's life for one's friends" (John 15:13).*
> *Prompted and led by my coworkers a fundraiser was held at the local park that yielded just over $1700. We are touched by each of those who gave of their time and demonstrated altruism. Throughout this whole experience I truly believe that a re-found faith in humanity has been restored for many. We have been contacted by people from out of state, pastors from multiple churches, acquaintances, friend's moms and dads and neighbors, and classmates.*

> *Even the police officer has stayed in touch as well as the EMS responders.*
> *Twelve hours without ventilator he will need to reach seventy-two then get capped, and we wait seventy-two more.*

My friend, Shawnn Parr, wrote to me, "Can't wait for the post when he comes home… You seem to be growing from this journey, rather than being beaten by it. Not taking anything for granted, I admire you for that." Still on another time, she wrote again to me, "I have actually prayed more in the last month than I have in a very long time." And finally sometime after, "Praying for him had also got me more in the habit of praying so that has been fantastic too." My heart went out to her who was battling her own injuries and setbacks.

> *Good will produces an aura of protection. I've said this before, we are all just one post from an unexpected journey, from a happy moment to what just happened. Todd and I have talked a lot about how we never realized this, nor that…that was until now.*
> *Living it is much different that knowing it is happening to someone else.*
> *Thank you, thank you.*
> *"Those who refresh themselves be refreshed" (Proverbs 11:25).*

June 29, 2015

> *"To this end, I strenuously contend with all my energy Christ so powerfully works me" (Colossians 1:29).*
> *Seven weeks tomorrow. Forty-nine days.*

This weekend was rough, the start of a new week, the stride continues.

I constantly remind myself that time is nothing, having Grant still with our family everything. Willing my brain to say blessed beyond words.

Weary a feeling and homesick a state of mind. Using muscles Grant hasn't used for weeks has made his back very sore, the pain making it hard for him to want to do any work. He lies and lies some more. Nausea and daily battle, his body as the doctor says, struggling to adjust, to recommit to life, to food, to function. Coughing through the trach is a struggle, bowels are a struggle, and pain is a struggle.

Today, he said, "Mom, I am so tired of being sick." This is the second time he has said this to me the same alligator tears I have been wiping since he was a toddler start to fall. I softly brush them away and say, "I know." Knowing he is doing all he can and his body just won't allow it is frustrating. Knowing also that the progress he needs can only be defined by him I say, "You have to do this, only you."

I stare out the window, summer half over, the outdoors call my name and all I can do is watch the sunlight stream through.

Day by day, minute by minute, time—in addition to the buzzes, beeps, and pressure sounds—is literally tick tock, tick tock.

In Romans 5: 3–4, "More than that, we rejoice in sufferings, knowing that suffering produces endurance produces character, character produces hope."

HOPE: Hold On the Pain Ends.

July 1, 2015

> *"Sometimes the wheel turns slowly but it still turns" (Lorne Michael).*
>
> *Took him off vent today and capped the trach. Goal one was to change to a smaller one (trauma put the larger one in) but when they went to take it out, it had been in so long, the tissue had healed around it and when they tried it wouldn't come out. They initially told us that an ENT would have to surgically remove it. This would hold up Goal two's progress.*
>
> *Grant became discouraged to which I said, "God hasn't left you left, he won't leave you now."*
>
> *Goal two: make it 8 hours off the collar with it capped. He made it 3, he needs 72 straight.*
>
> *Last week getting of the vent to the collar he did 45 minutes, the next day 4 hours, the next 12 and then capped at 30.*
>
> *Three is our 45 today, blessed.*
>
> *Grant is doing all he can, all his body will allow.*
>
> *"I think a hero is an ordinary individual who finds strength to persevere and endure in spite of overwhelming circumstances" (Christopher Reeve).*

Trach procedure would be done later this day. Darnell, the respiratory therapist said he could do it. Grant's head and neck were lifted off the bed when he pulled. Grant's neck was also bleeding, but once the new one was replaced, Grant could already breathe better. He said, the first, larger, emergent trach was likely to be what was holding us up. Grant could not get any air around the larger trach, which would have possibly expedited its earlier removal.

July 3, 2015

Thank you for the immediate prayers! I told Grant that God would take care of him!

Trach changed, he was so brave. They said wait until tomorrow to start capping again.

There was another boy in an accident shortly after Grant's. We followed his story through his girlfriend. Grant said he wanted to let them know he was thinking of them. I told him to look on her page and comment. I said, "Isn't this our Grant?"

"Helping others is not a choice, it is a purpose" (Prophetess Andrea).

Other than the Father's Day picture, this was the second day I posted a picture throughout it all. Not because I didn't want to but because I knew that Grant was owed some dignity throughout this process, and I would have wanted the same thing if it were me. This was the first day Grant was given more time outside. He stayed capped with his trach for eight hours before they hooked him back up to the ventilator. Grant loved to be outside. He loved the sun and its warmth. He embraced the fresh air and just to be able to be free. Summer was and always had been his favorite season. He loved to sit outside. He could feel progress, too, and this was instrumental.

We had a picnic outside in the garden area.

"I'm singing at the top of my lungs, I'm so full of answered prayers" (Psalm 13:6).

Picnic in the garden, cap on goal today 8 hours! First day in a T-shirt in almost 8 weeks.

July 5, 2015

> *"So I say to you, ask and will be given unto you: seek and you shall find: knock and the door will be opened unto you" (Luke 11:9).*
>
> *For fifty-five days Grant has either had a tube down his throat or in his trach in, today the trach was removed. He is breathing fine on his own with minimal oxygen. Also coming in soon to remove his central line.*
>
> *Hoping that we are home by mid-week. What a blessing today is! Hearing him, seeing his great big smile…simply blessed beyond words.*
>
> *Thank you, thank you, and thank you! Every prayer lifted is why we are where we are. God has heard our prayers and answered them.*
>
> *"If opportunity does not knock and present itself, you beat the door down."*
>
> *Today sweet friends, Grant beat the door down!*

I think this was the day I felt there was power, not just power in prayer or power in faith but a control. For several months, everything had made me powerless in every way until I felt I had gained control over the situation, and it was elating. I felt that Grant had conquered this and that he, too, felt in control. Not only could he demonstrate that he had control, but he could also verbalize it.

July 6, 2015

> *First and foremost, all the praise, honor, and glory be given unto God. "I am the vine, you are the branches, he who abides in me and I in him he bears much fruit, for apart from me you can do nothing" (John 15:5).*
>
> *Countless hours spent on bended knee and countless people uplifting prayers. "If we are together,*

nothing is impossible. If we are divided, we fail" (Winston Churchill).

There are no words to adequately express our deepest gratitude for everything that each of you have done for us.

So from the words of Napoleon Bonaparte, "A picture is worth a thousand words."

And I posted my final third picture with Grant holding his dry-erase board saying "Going home."

After we arrived home, Grant continued outpatient care throughout November. He still had open belly wounds that required wound care, and so once a week, we took him in to have a new plan. Many kinds of materials were placed on his wounds, and then they were covered. Each was trying to heal and allowing the skin to regrow. He also had two months of physical therapy to regain his strength. More shots, more medications. He was home, and that was all that mattered. Recovery was still part of the plan, and he could do that. Grant also needed to rebuild muscle and weight. He saw his primary care doctor once weekly. He had to get some injections required since he had lost his spleen; most of it became routine. Most of his doctors told us to wait a year before we could expect him to be remotely better. By the anniversary of his accident, he was doing great unless he pulled his shirt up and one could see the scars. One would never know the journey this young man had been on.

A year and a half after his accident, his dad said to him, "Thank you, Grant. Thank you for being so strong." Still more than a year later, I was in my office one morning. En route to work, I had received a phone call from a friend who had told me about a high school classmate whose son was in a terrible accident, life-lined and critical. She asked me to pray and to reach out. As much as I tried all morning to get on track, I struggled. The next day, our trauma team sent out a request to show acknowledgment for a peer who went above. One therapist could sense I was struggling. Her timing was impeccable when I wrote this:

Yesterday on my way into the office, I received a call from high school classmates. This call was to tell me that another high school classmate son, 19, had been involved in a terrible car accident and he was not expected to make it. I got into my office, closed the door, and knelt to pray while the tears fell. Knowing all too well what that knock on the door or late-night phone call felt like, it was a parent's worst nightmare.

I continued to cry on my desk through most of the morning, unable to concentrate on anything as my mind had flashbacks of when my own son's accident occurred. Those feelings of guilt, those familiar feelings of immense fear of the unknown deep sadness and unbelievable stress. I closed my door and just sat silently, absorbing all of this but knowing I was at work and had to stay on task. I just sat in the room, thankful, for nothing was too important that I didn't have to give 100 percent, 75 percent at best.

Back to my office to retreat, I allowed the silent tears to fall in quietness of my *own place* in this office. Then I made a computer error (surprise). I enlisted a therapist who came over to help me. She could tell I seemed bothered. She asked if I was okay, but I just wanted to tell her how badly my heart was hurt for D'Lee, how much all the pain and fear I had experienced with my Grant was in front of me. Megan sat there and let me say it, and she just listened. Then she said, "Can I hug you?" For about five minutes, she just held on to me. She allowed me to feel the pain to relive the trauma and to let me just know that I was okay now that my nightmare was over. After about five minutes (intense sobbing), I could hear her voice gently saying, "You are safe. Grant is safe. You are here with me." I felt better, I actually felt better. I was able to tell her how bad I was hurt, and she just stayed in that moment with me no matter what other responsibilities she had.

More than a year later, it was right there in front of me, in front of my face. My heart was vulnerable as it happened since May 12, 2015, until this day on October 10, 2016. I am reminded that I am changed, that I was changed, that who I used to be was who I will never be again. I am different now.

When I started this book, I went back, way back—back to a time in my life where not only my heart was so dark but so was my vision. Whether it was a sunny day or a room full of people, I spent my life walking blinded. I allowed my fears, my past losses, my insecurities, and, most of all, the devil to rob me of my life. I made excuses, I covered myself in a blanket of isolation and loneliness, and I allowed myself to fear that others would judge me. I didn't enjoy gatherings of any kind. I avoided them. I didn't speak unless asked to speak too. I had lived my life for so long. Being alone was all I knew. I taught social skills for a living but didn't really have them myself. *Unsocial* wasn't just a word; it was who I was.

I spent my weekends with my nose in a book or watching chick flicks. I often headed to the store only to turn the car around. I was unable to force myself to go anywhere. I just wanted to be home. I had spent years holding my breath, wondering where the boys were and if they were coming home, being interrogated daily by Todd, withholding information to spare him the misery that I had to endure when they passed curfew or broke down, and suffering silently with the secrets I was forced to keep. I felt abandoned, forgotten. My confidence was stripped long, long ago, lost even back in my high school days, and I had never gotten it back. But I felt safe with my kids in my own home.

I used to tell my mom that I felt safest between my bookshelves. I also carried big bags of books. Some I never opened, some I had read several times over. They were like good friends. I felt safe when I was with them. I even carried one in my purse. Metaphorically speaking, it was like carrying a loaded gun. I still do this. I once read a book about taking thirty minutes a day just for you and if you had that thirty minutes what you would do. I wrote to read. Books made me happy. The time in the hospital allowed me the time to read, to dig deep into my faith, to study more about God's Word, to draw closer to him. The books, they slowed me down.

For everyone else, Grant's accident brought love and faith. Prayer was a part of daily living—make that *hourly* living. Although there were many dark days, God allowed the sun to shine again day after day. He opened and healed a broken heart, he restored lost faith, and he guided me. All those times I thought I was alone, but I never really was. Job 42:15 said, "My ears have heard of you but now my eyes have seen you."

Sometime during the rough draft phase of this book, I shared it with my husband. I handed it to him with joy in my heart and said, "Here you go."

I said, "It's the good, the bad, and the ugly, but it's all me."

A few days later, as our schedules rarely connected, I asked what he thought of the book. He said, "That was depressing."

Once again, I felt condemned.

For months I had reviewed journals, researched, poured myself into something I was hopeful would help someone else. Instead, the one person I knew would understand would remind me once again, "Maybe you just aren't good enough." (He felt bad). Even still in this time, we had family come in once again. The days of the visit were on a shortened timetable. They were to come on a Sunday. I stayed up almost the whole night to prepare old pictures and food. When it was time for them to come, they canceled. I had enough food for an army and went to bagging it to freeze. As the tears fell most of the day, I heard the devil said to me, "You are not good enough. They do not like you. That is why they did not come." I could not make sense of them avoiding us, as I had tried so hard to have the perfect day. Instead, I decided to do something else. This book really wasn't about me. It wasn't really about my trials and the tribulations of myself or of my family that we had conquered. It was about something more. Something far greater. God led my heart, and I followed him.

I read a devotional by Amy Carroll. She told a story about a friend who shared her story about abortion. Fearing for sharing her story would change Amy's perception of her, she was worried about telling it. In contrast, Amy told a different story. She said, "We transparently share our stories of his work in our lives. Your life isn't perfect, neither is mine!" So did I embarrass myself by putting my story out there? No, I was beyond blessed that I served a risen Savior who gave me trials that make me who I am. If I could encourage you through my troubles, then my purpose was served. If I could help you understand that you are never alone, then I have served another purpose by writing.

You see, without them, I would have never had this story to write. Without them, I would never have had the ability to know how blessed I really was. They gave me the stage to stand on, to believe in myself, to believe in God, to know that they were the only audience I need to feel empowered. I didn't have to worry about all the people who should do the right thing and be kind. I only had to worry that I was the person I want to be.

> I observe that there are two different theories according to which individual men seek to get on in this world. One theory leads man to pull down everybody around him in order to climb to a higher place. The other leads man to help everybody around him in order that he may go up with them. (Elihu Root)

I want to be the latter. I want to work at being a better person than I was the day before. I want to lift others up and not to tear them down. I'm content to allow others to stand while I sit. It isn't about always being right, but it is about being able to listen and stay quiet. It is about being able to let someone else have the glory because as long as a person knows they are right, they have nothing to worry about.

Paraphrasing again from Amy, she goes on to say that we share our own stories to help others grow and heal. Just like Amy's friend, here is *our* story: the good and the not-so-good, but it is a reality of what was. For the first time in a long time, I was no longer in darkness; the light was shining through.

My hope for you is that, if you are struggling as I was, you are able to lay your burdens at God's feet and walk away. Turn the lights on and leave that dark room behind you. Am I there? Most likely I am not; none of us will ever *be there*. I read somewhere where we are all "unfinished works of art, in the art of being." I have a stressful job,

BREATHE

I work with stressful people, and my home life is always stressful. I say things I shouldn't, I make mistakes, I fall, and I get back up. I try to balance some of my inadequacies by making the right choice. Coping is something we have to remind ourselves to do daily. The difference now is that I walk in His light and not in my darkness, and I don't walk alone.

FOOTPRINTS IN THE SAND

One night I dreamed I was walking along the beach with the Lord. Many scenes from my life flashed across the sky.

In each scene I noticed footprints in the sand. Sometimes there were two sets of footprints, other times there was one only.

This bothered me because I noticed that during the low periods of my life, when I was suffering from anguish, sorrow or defeat, I could see only one set of footprints, so I said to the Lord,

"You promised me Lord, that if I followed you, you would walk with me always. But I have noticed that during the most trying periods of my life there has only been one set of footprints in the sand. Why, when I needed you most, have you not been there for me?"

The Lord replied, "The years when you have seen only one set of footprints, my child, is when I carried you."

—Mary Stevenson, 1936.

ABOUT THE AUTHOR

Katherine Daugherty graduated from Vincennes University with an AS degree in Social Work. She went on to Saint Mary of the Woods College and graduated with her BS degree and double major in Psychology and Human Services. Katherine has worked in the mental health field for almost fifteen years as well as with children and their families through most of her adult life. From substitute teaching to VBS, Bible studies, and PTO, Katherine actively engaged in her children's lives as they have grown. Her passions are her faith and her family. Katherine lives in Indiana with her husband, Todd, and their three grown children and their families. When she is not working or with her family, you will catch her either walking or reading.